Adult Coloring Book: Ma

Symphony

A Music Coloring Book for Heart, Mind and Soul

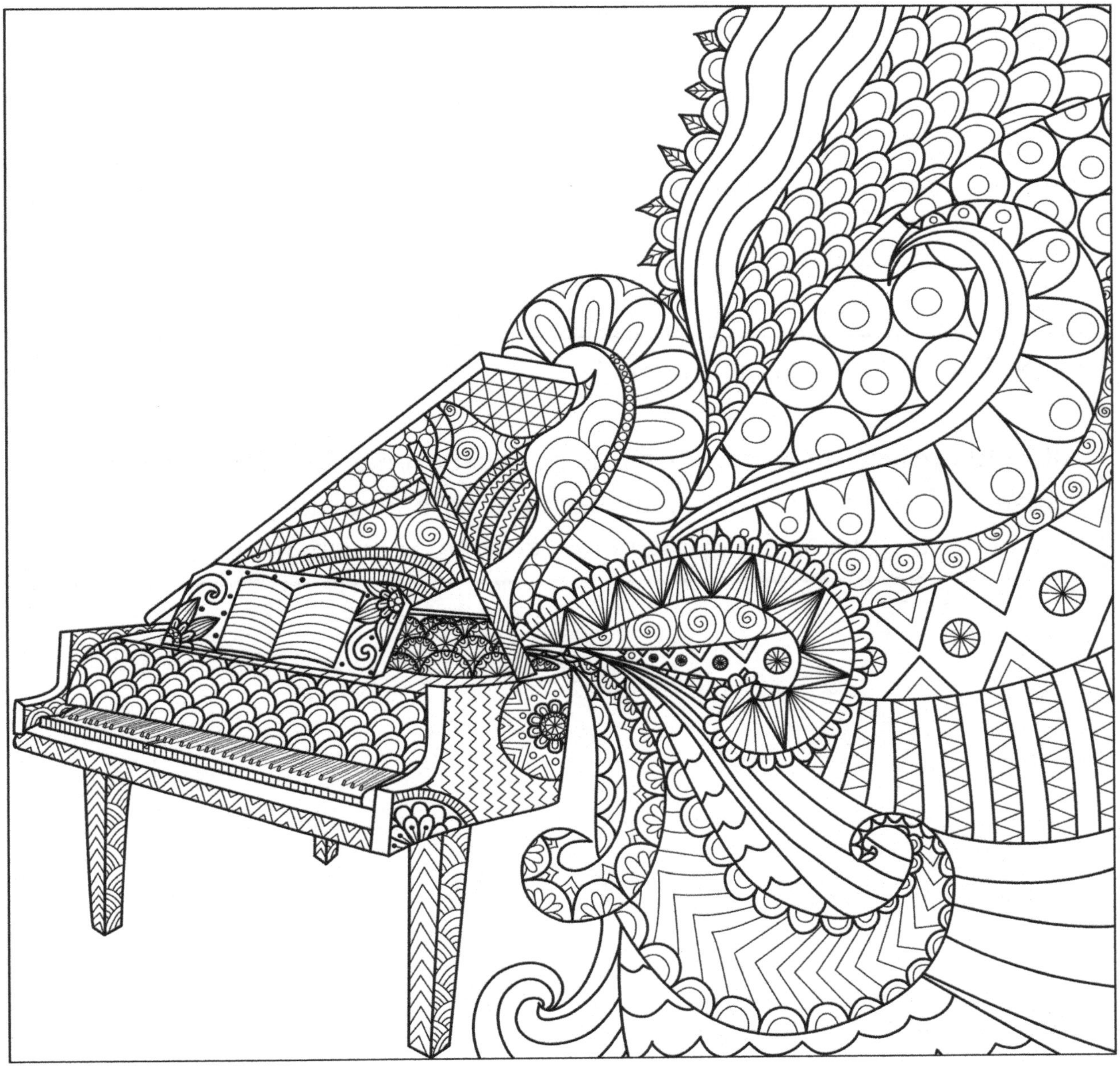

MantraCraft™

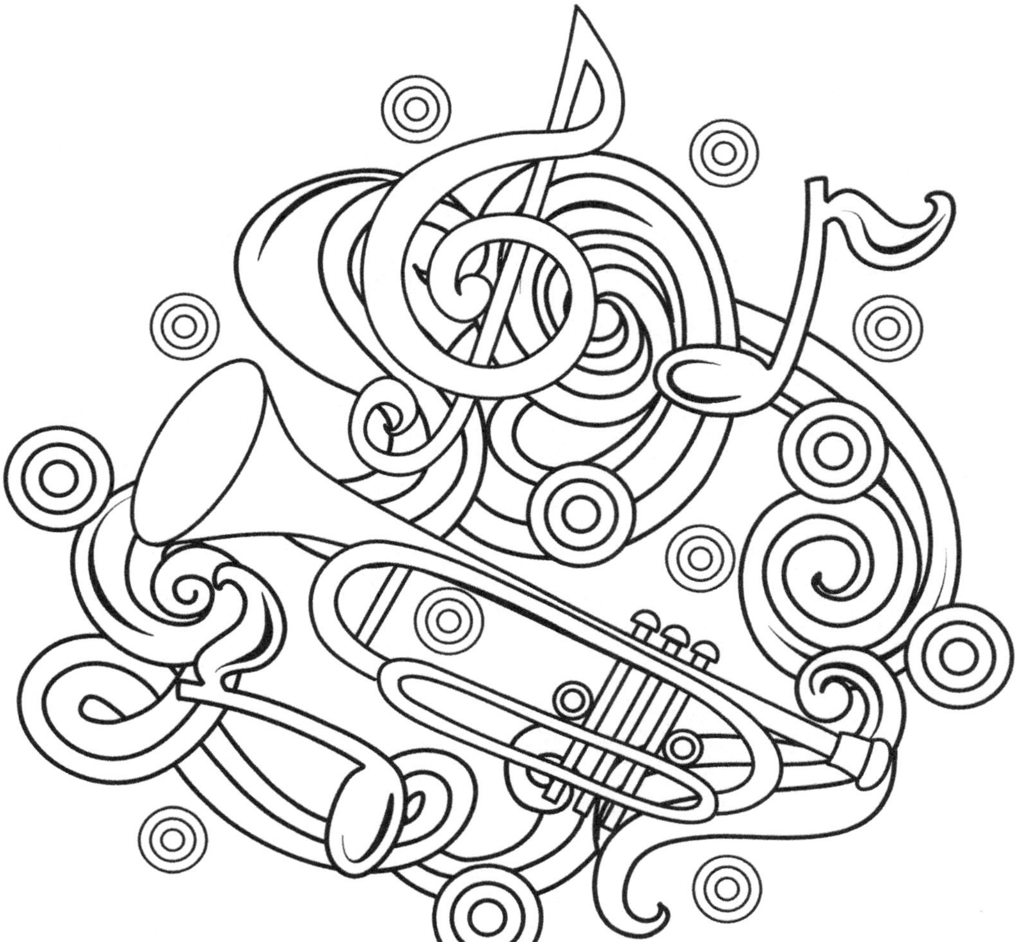

This Coloring Book belongs to:

Color Test Page

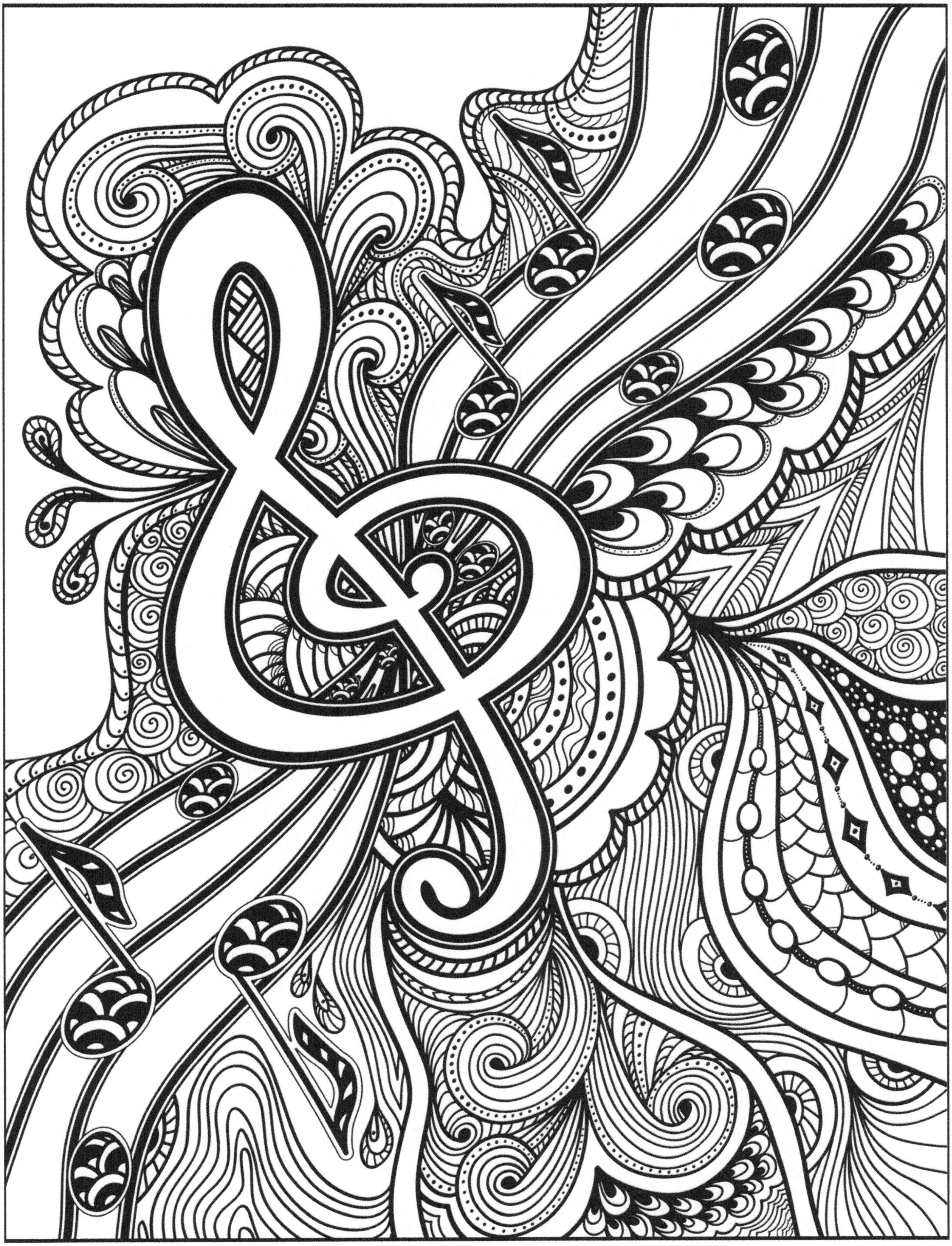

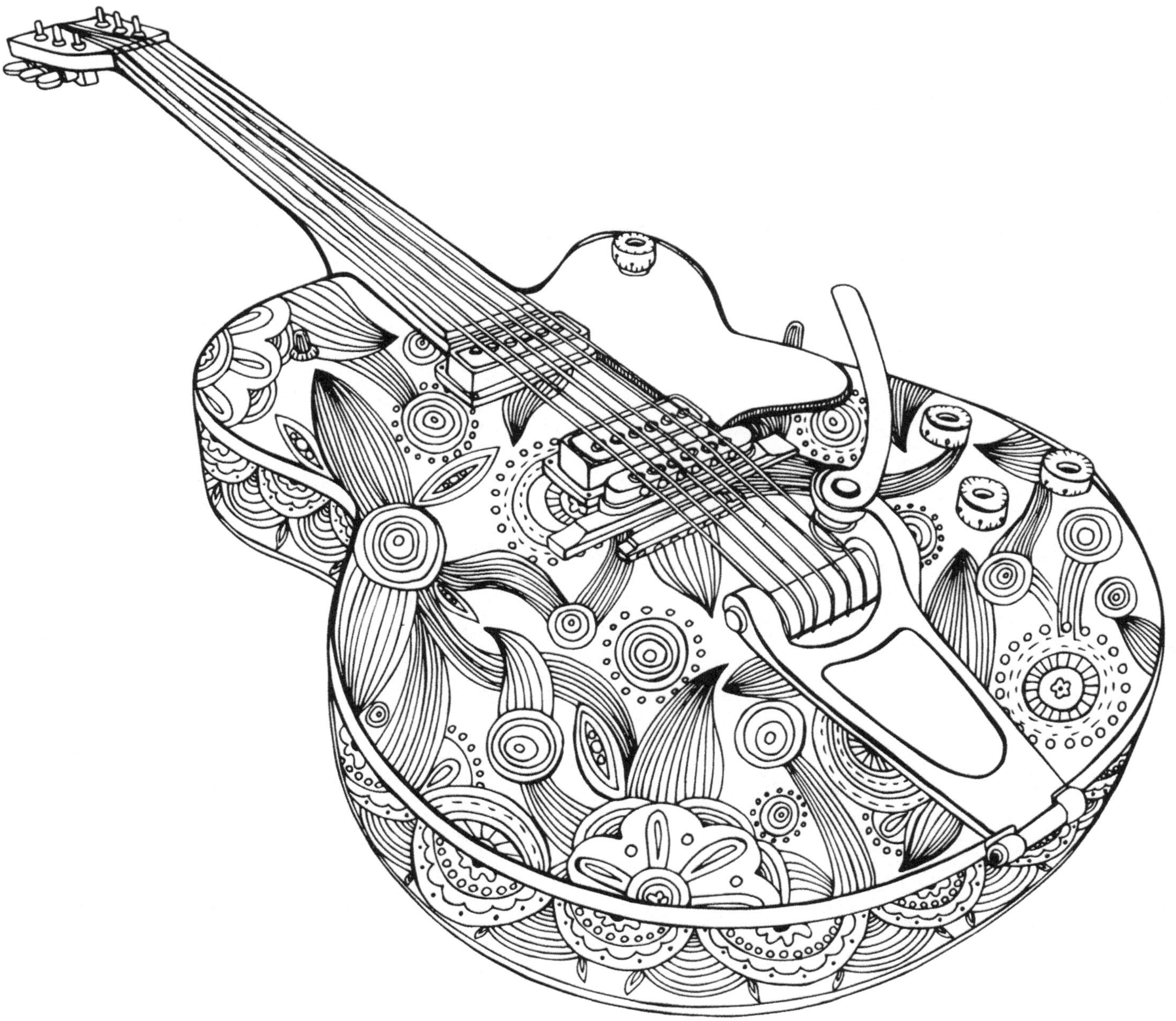

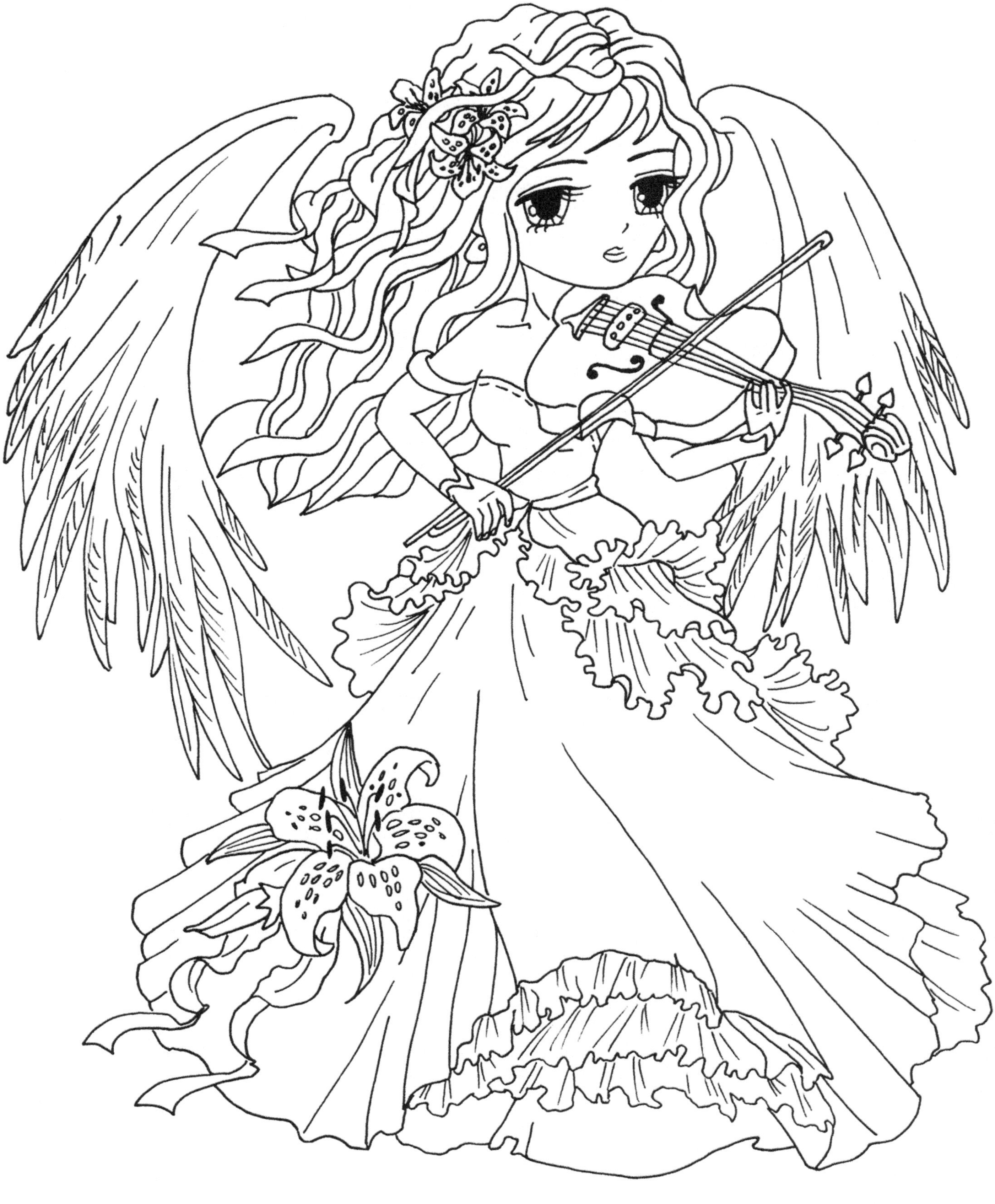

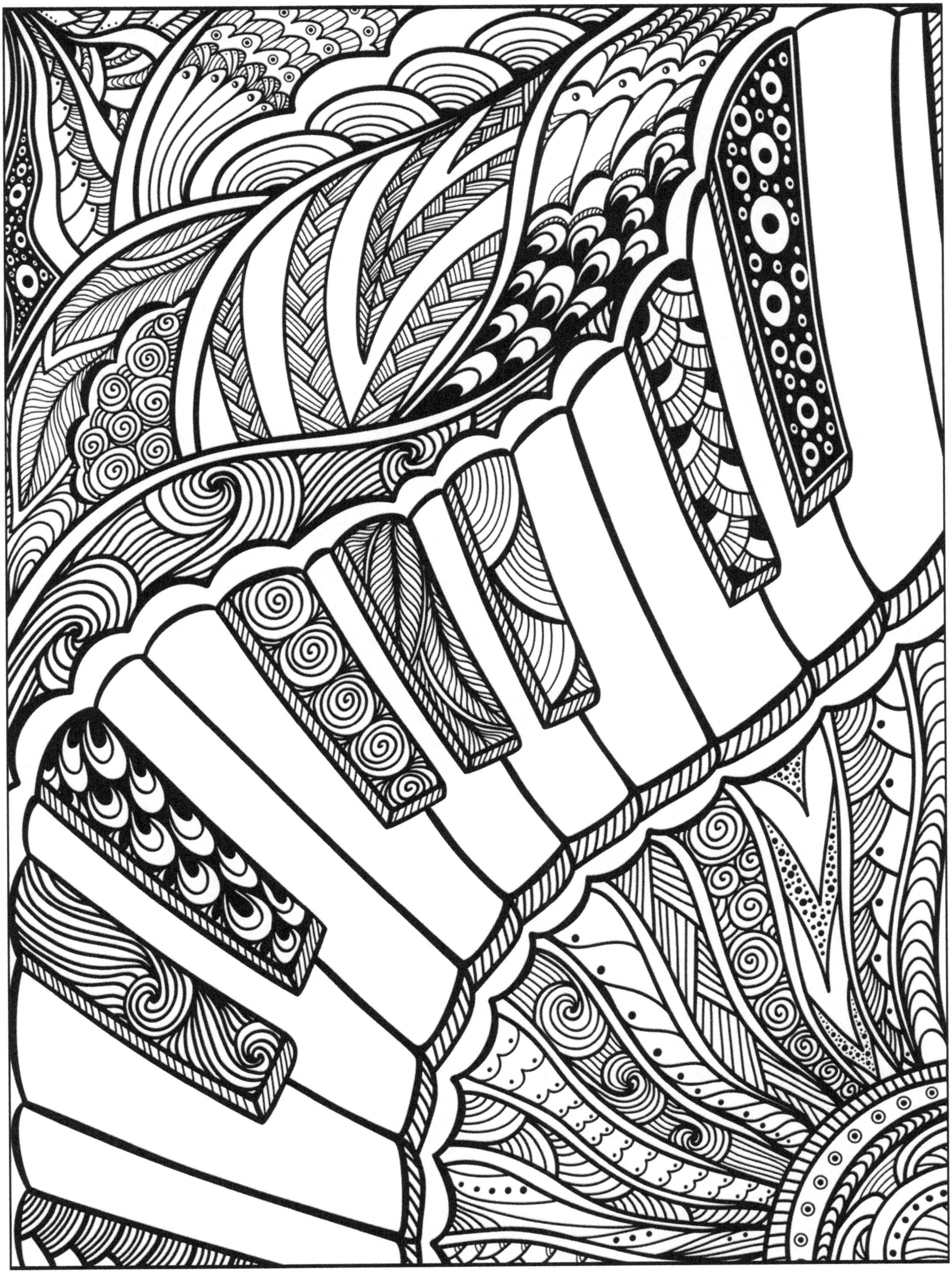

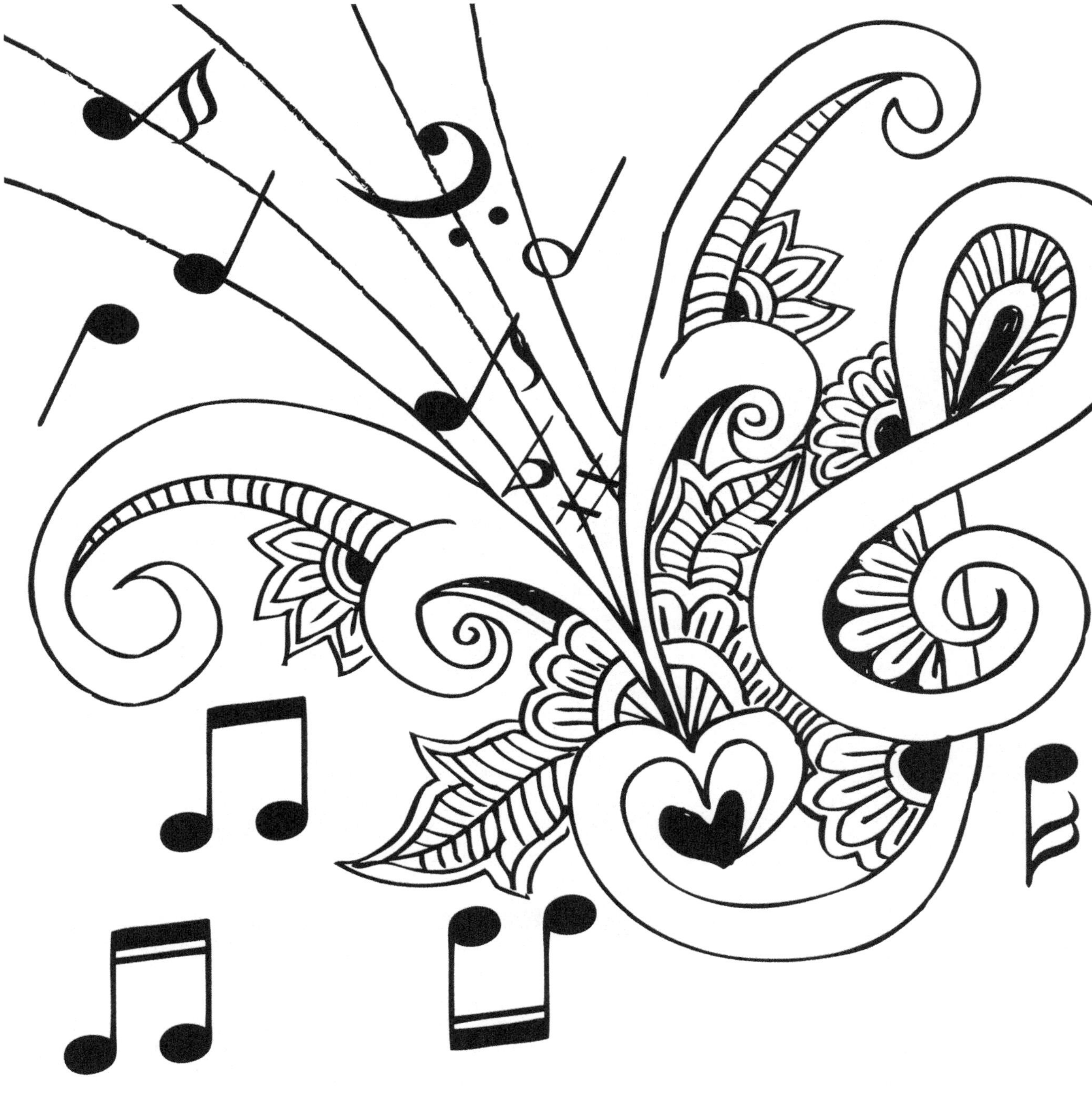

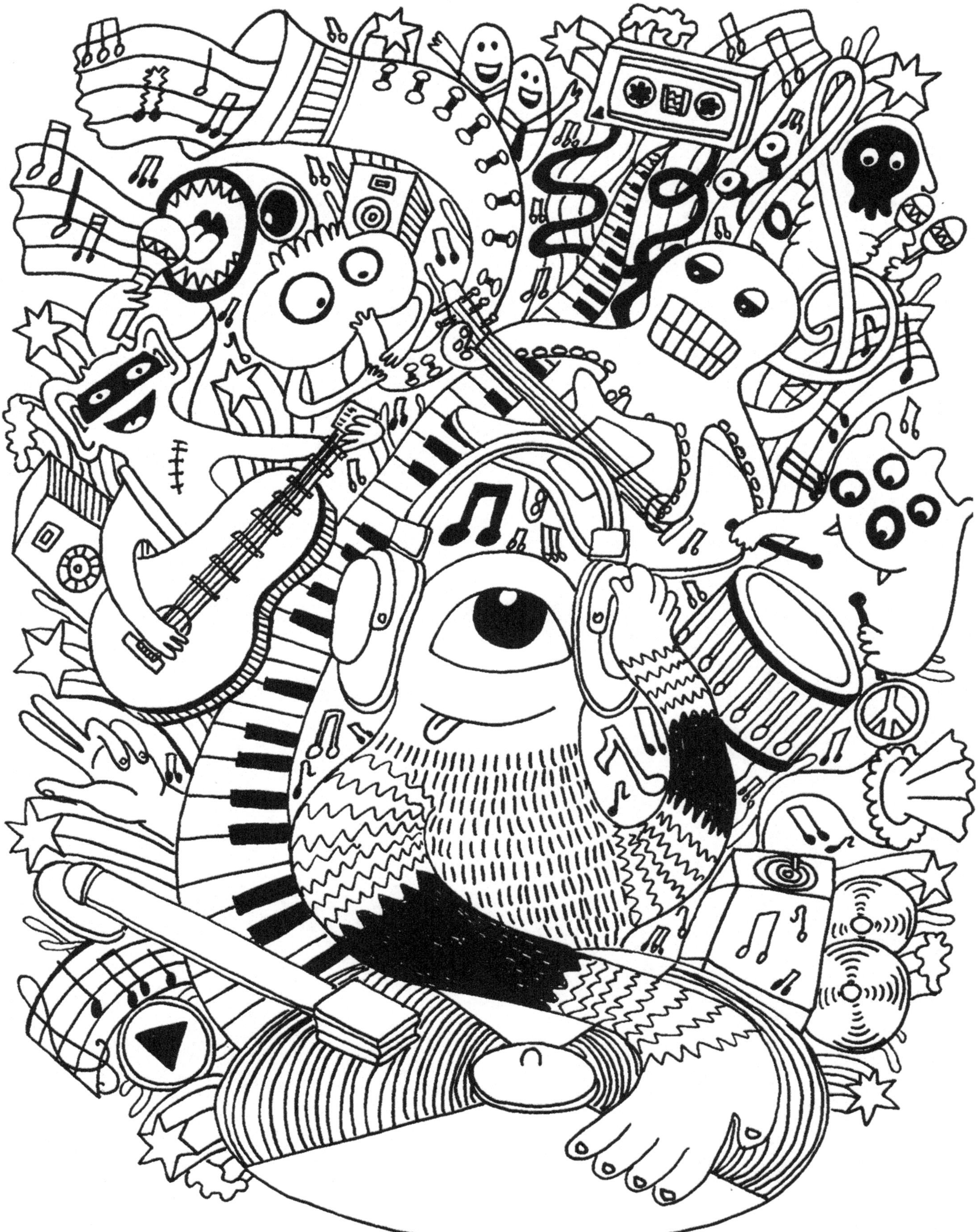

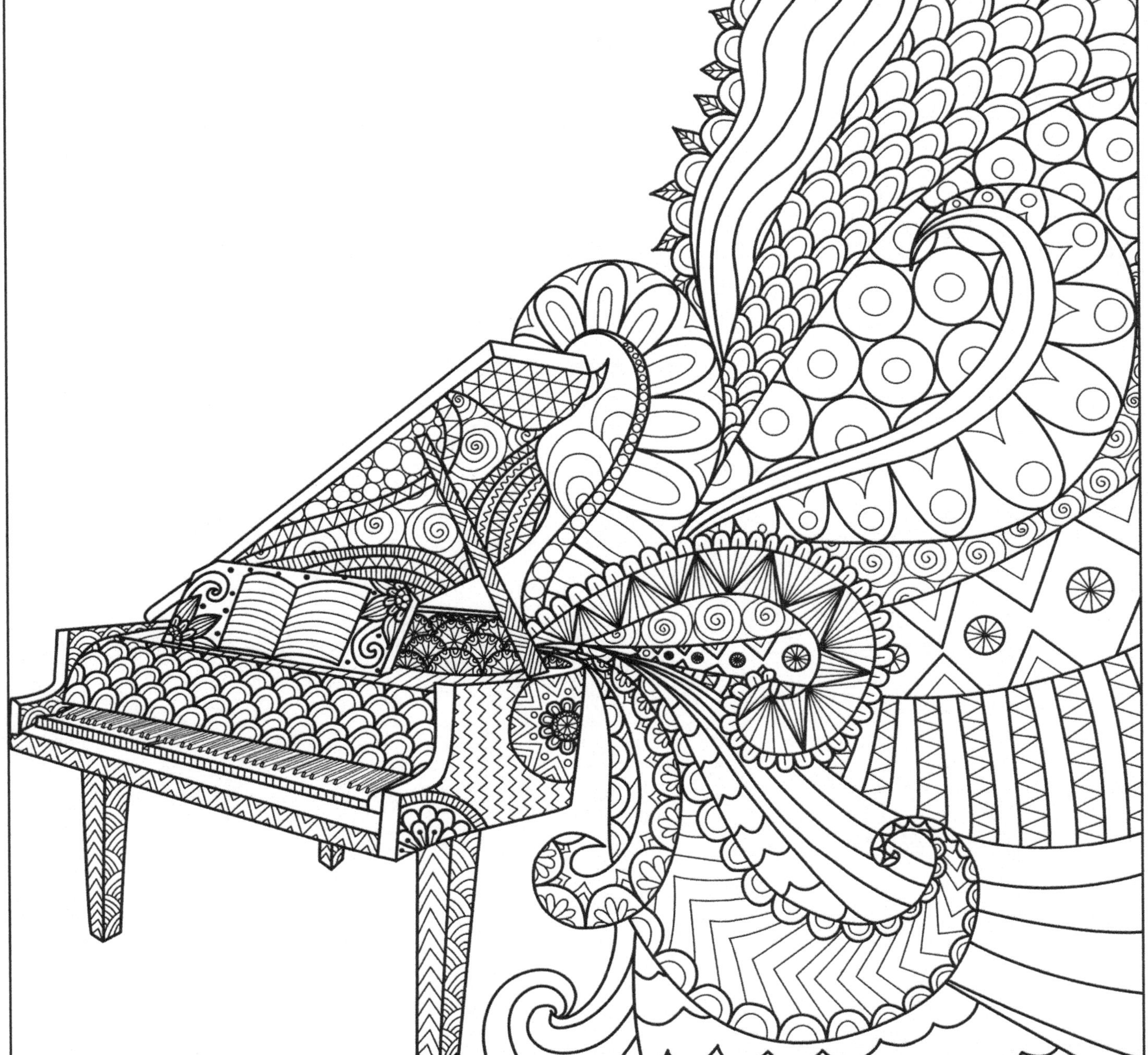

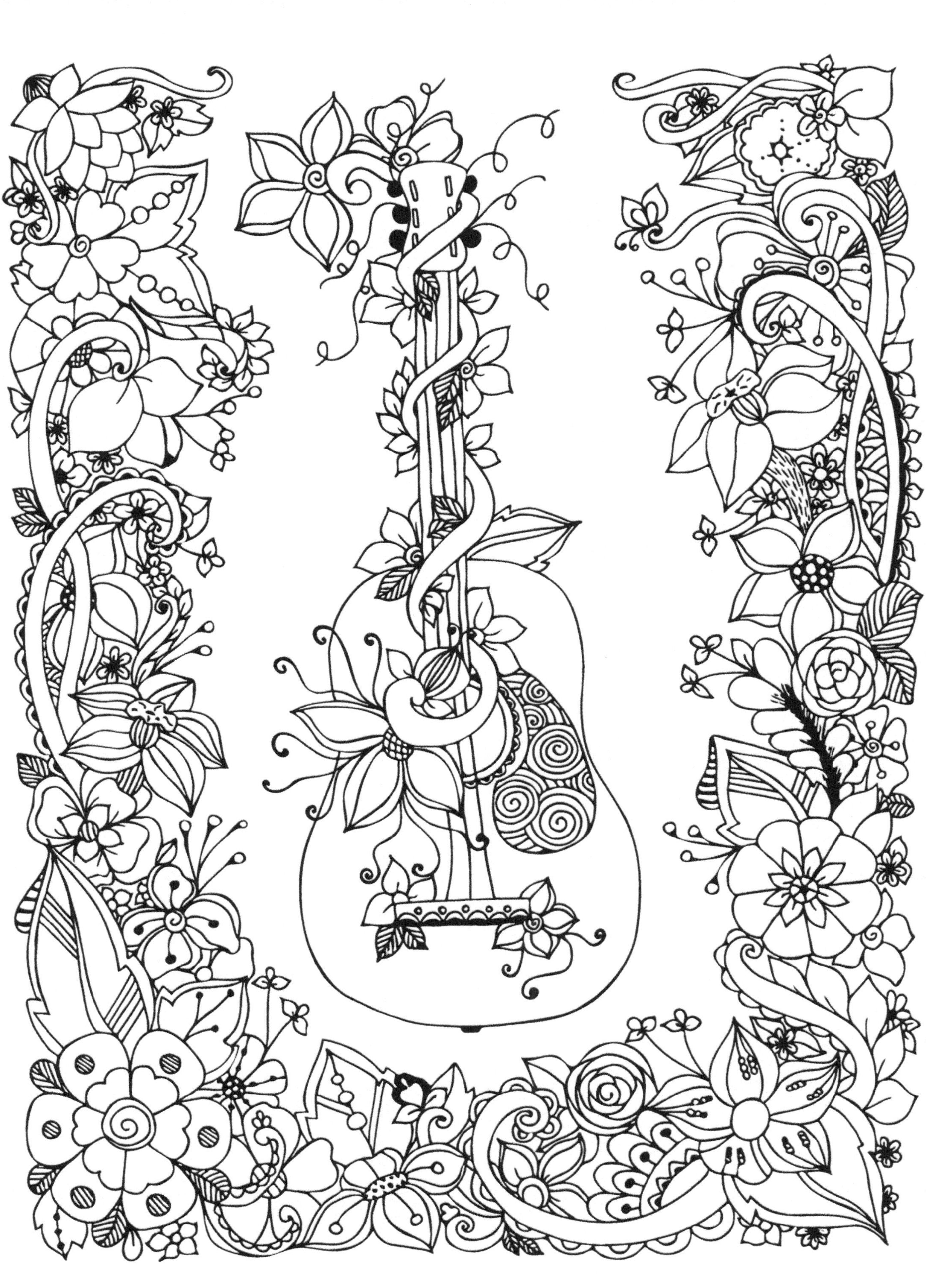

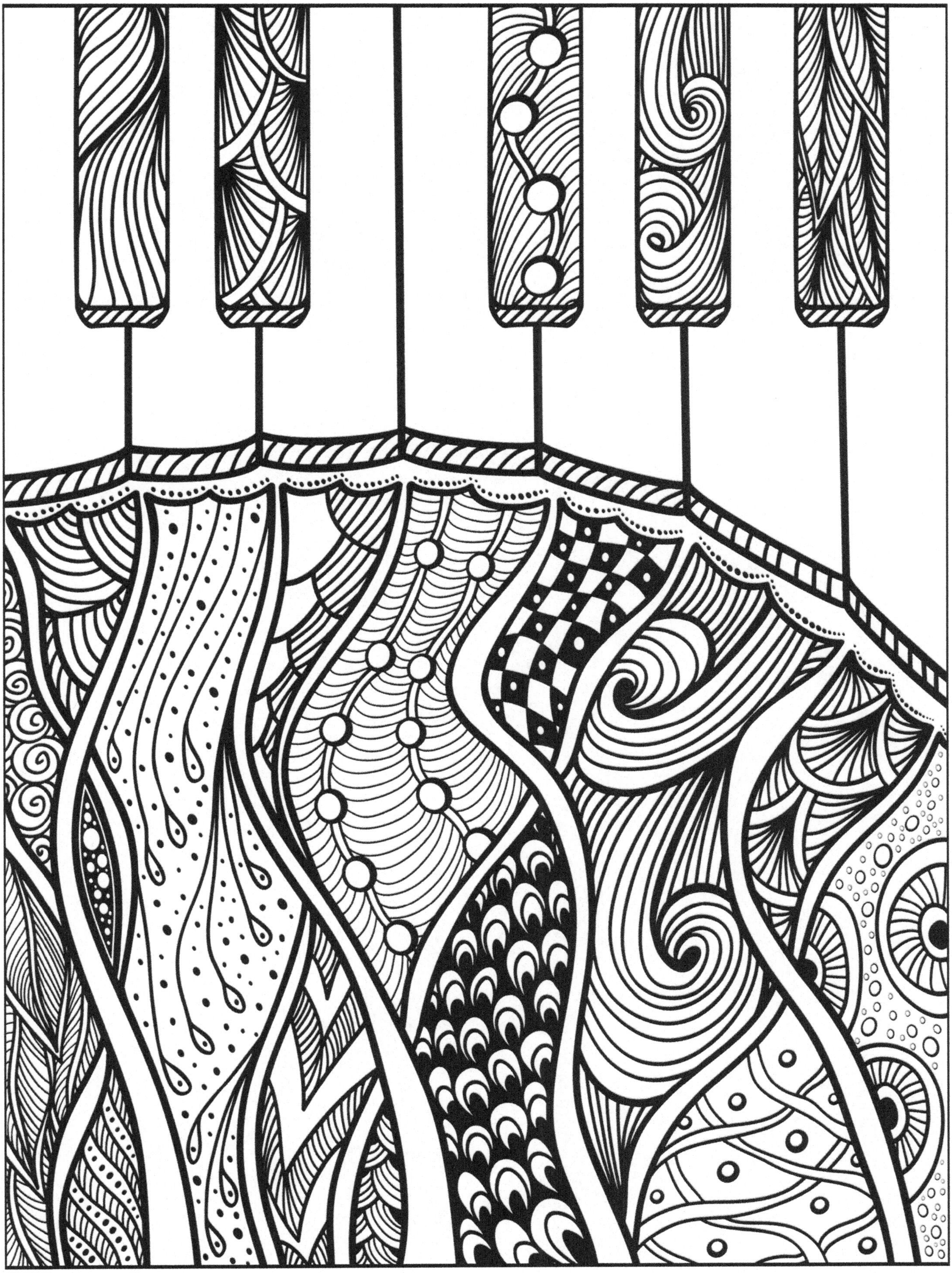

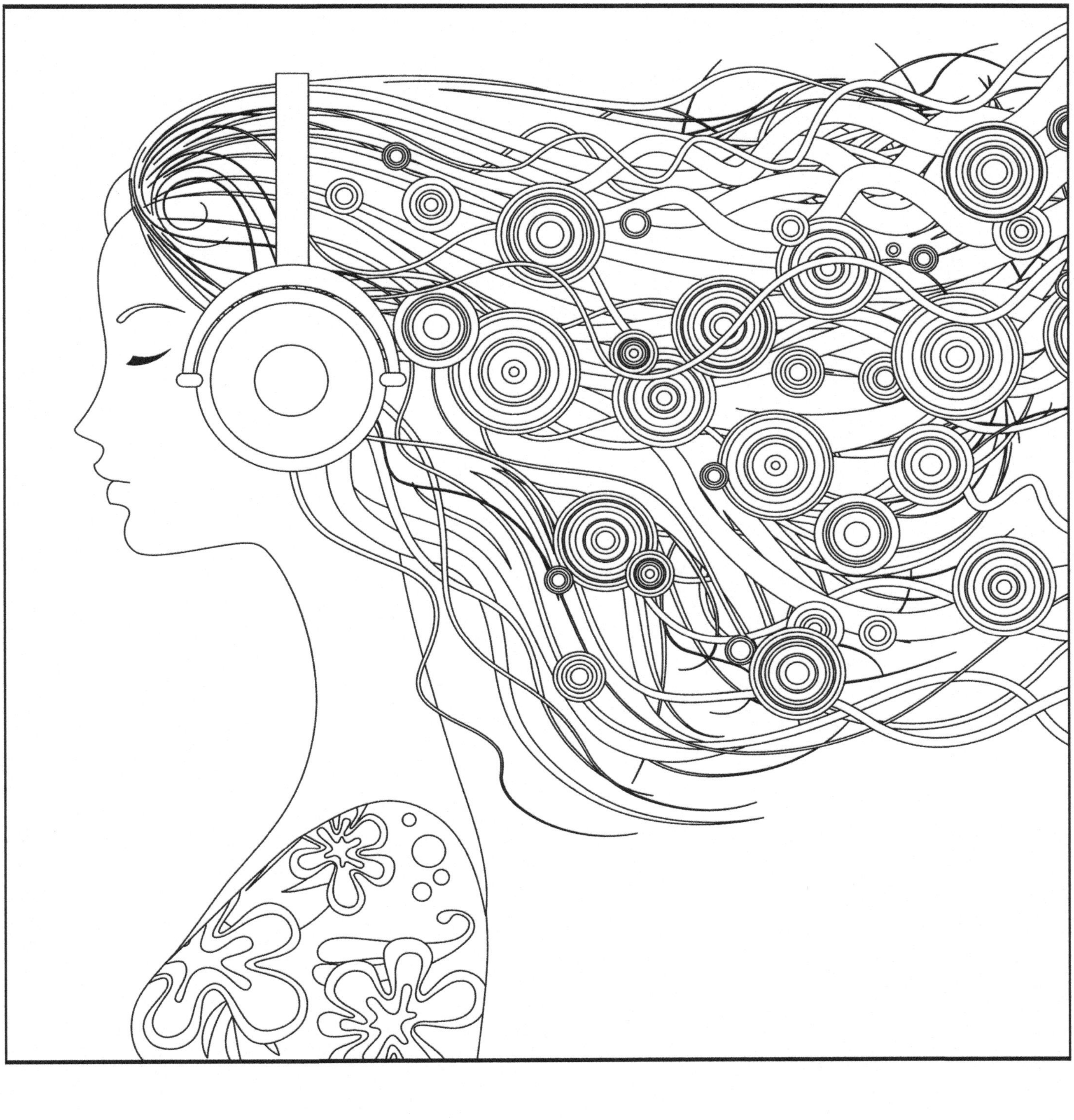

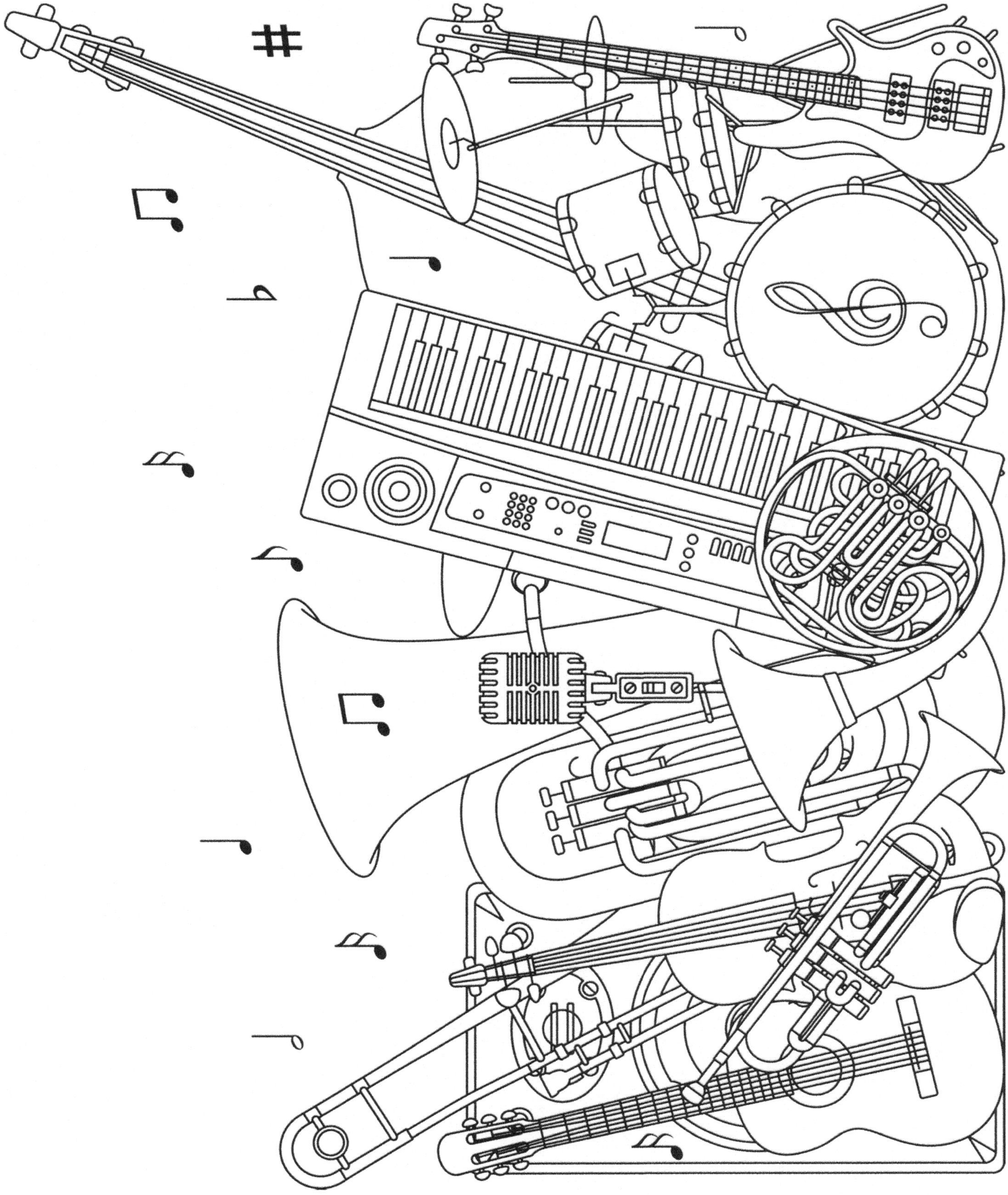

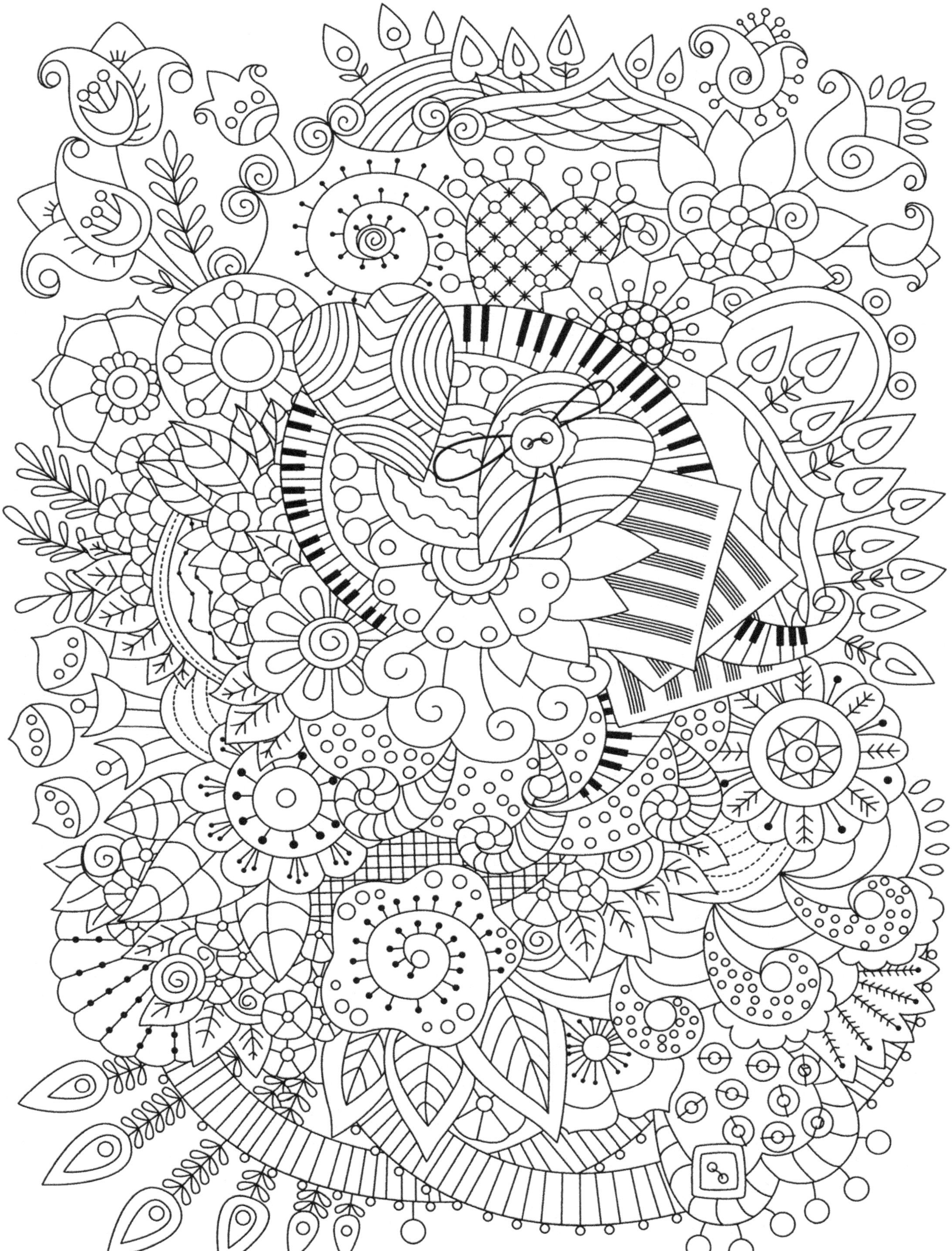

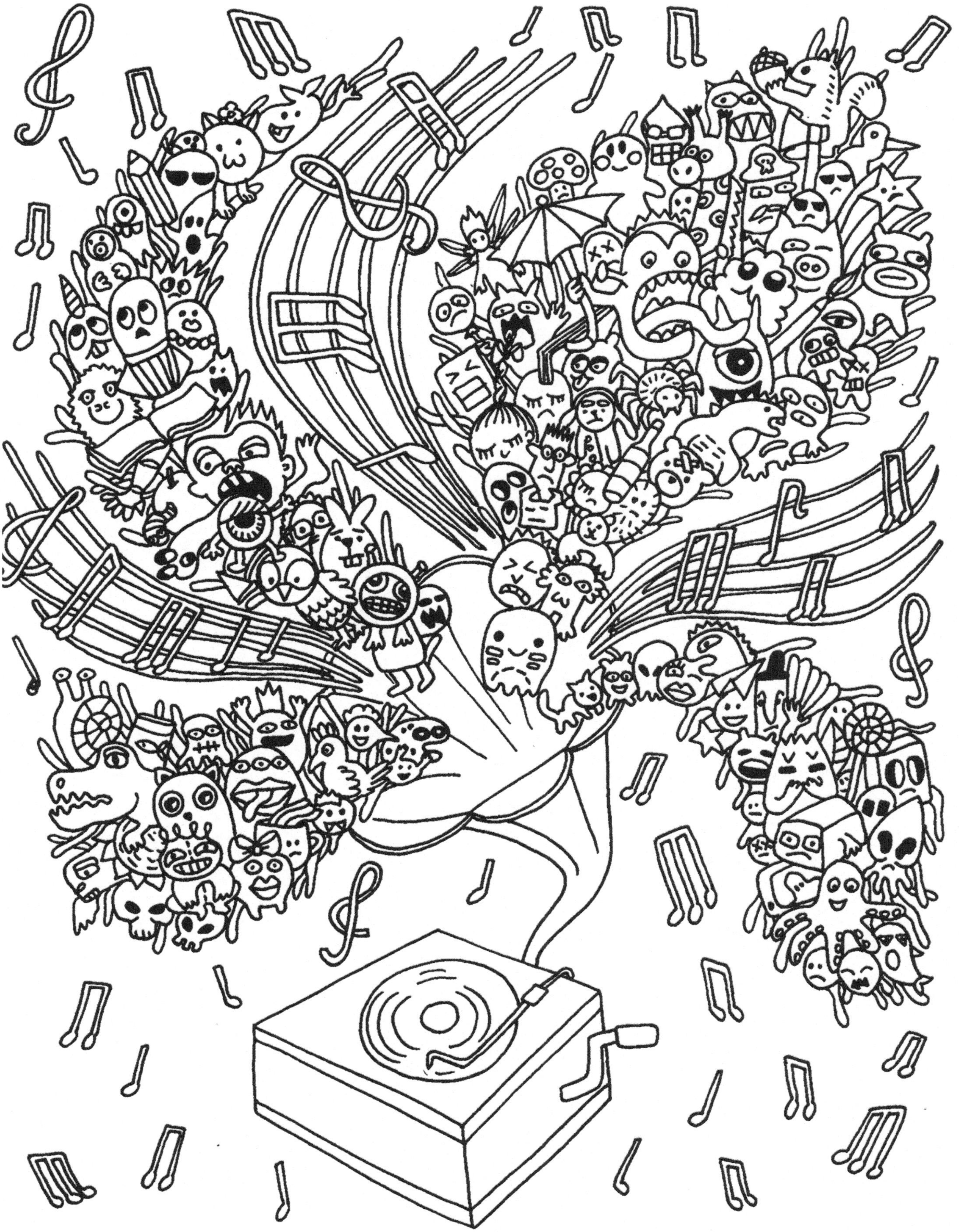

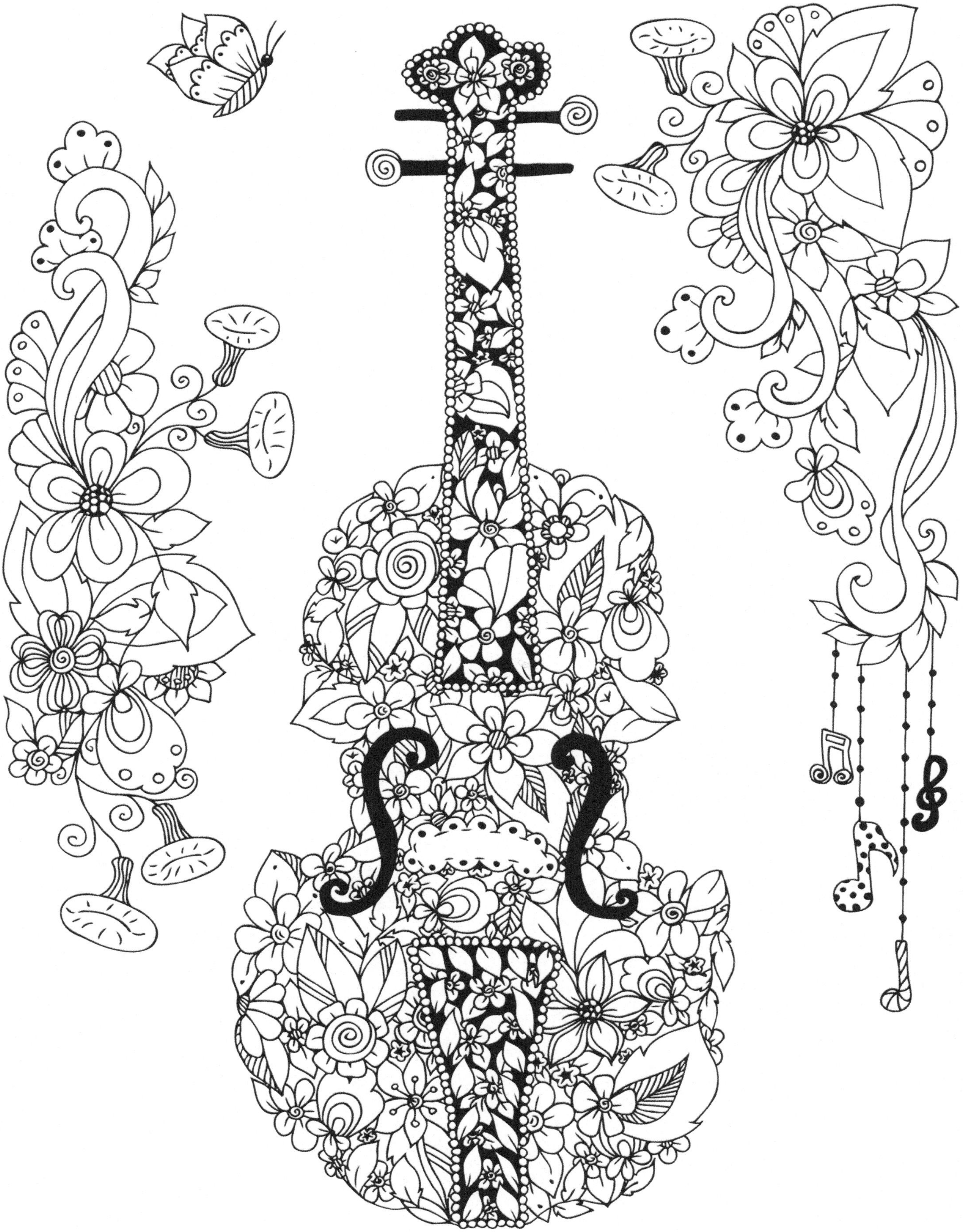

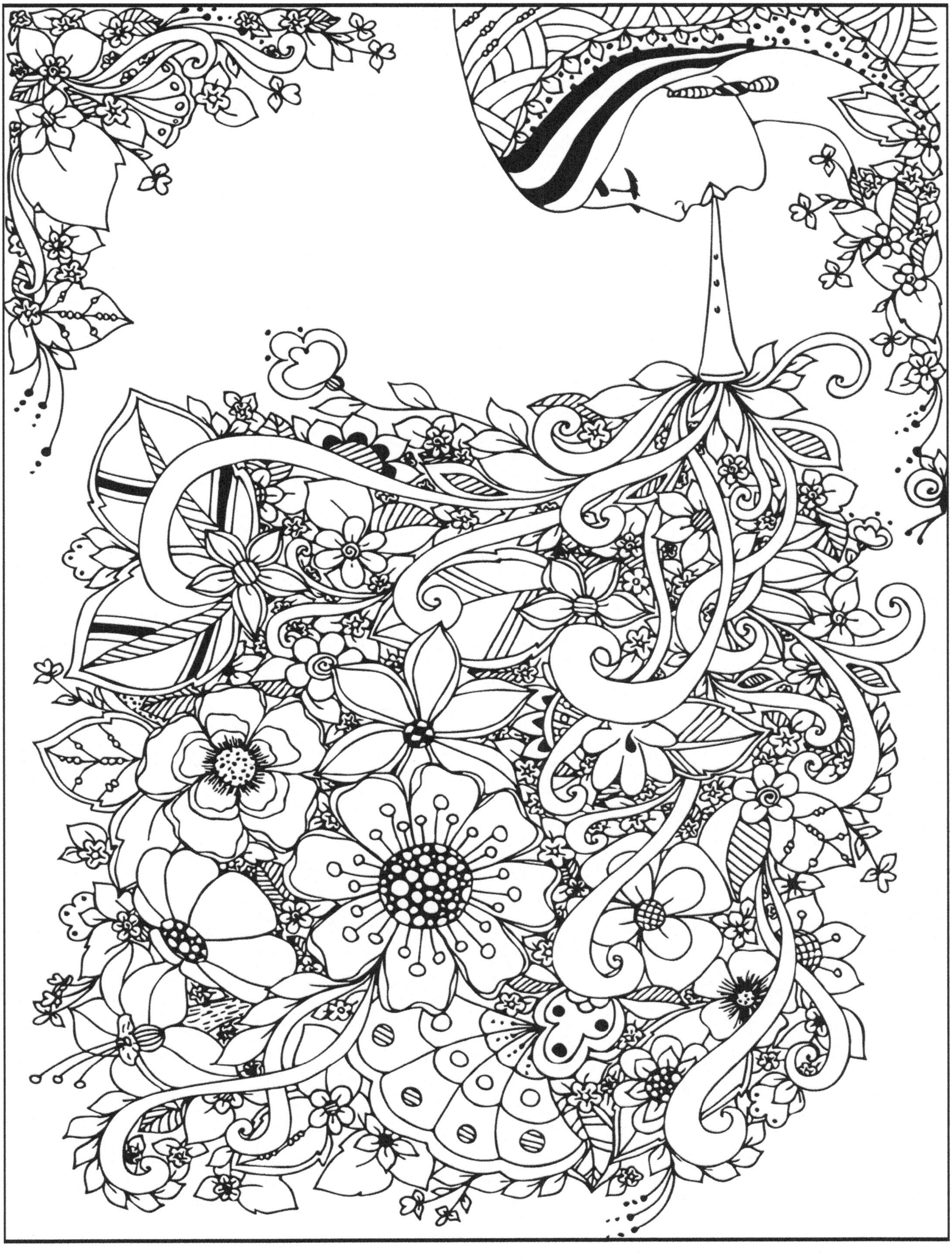

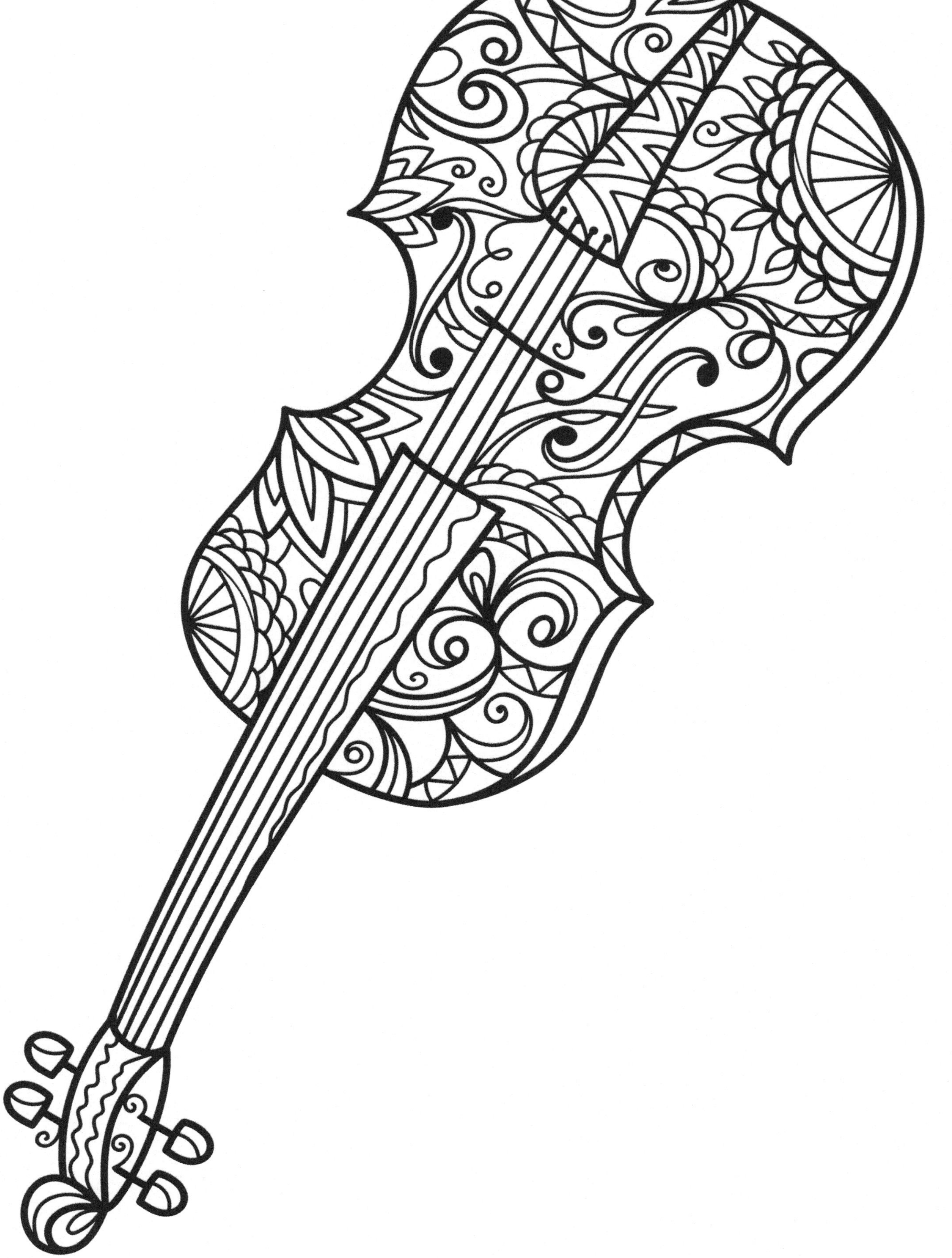

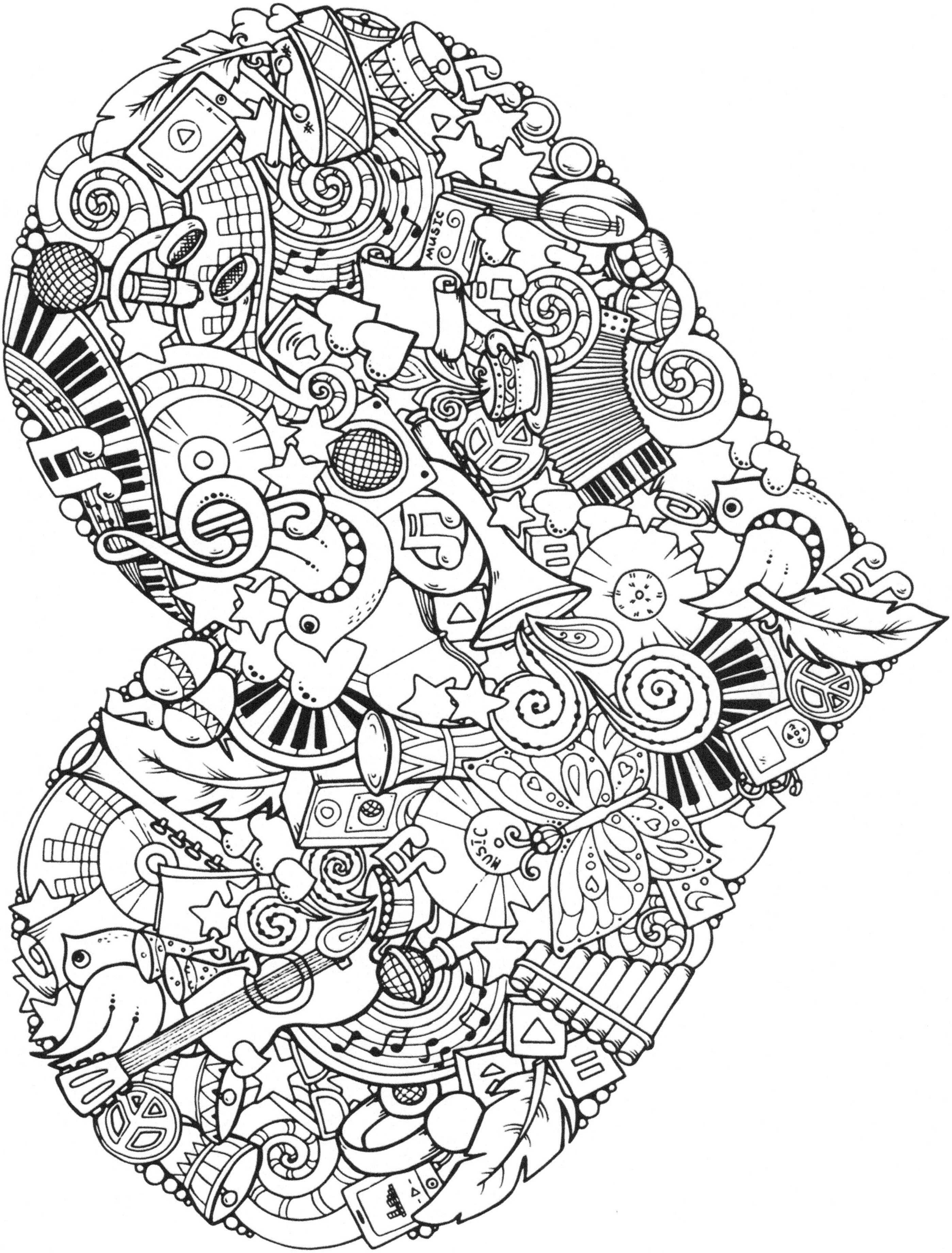
MUSIC
MUSIC

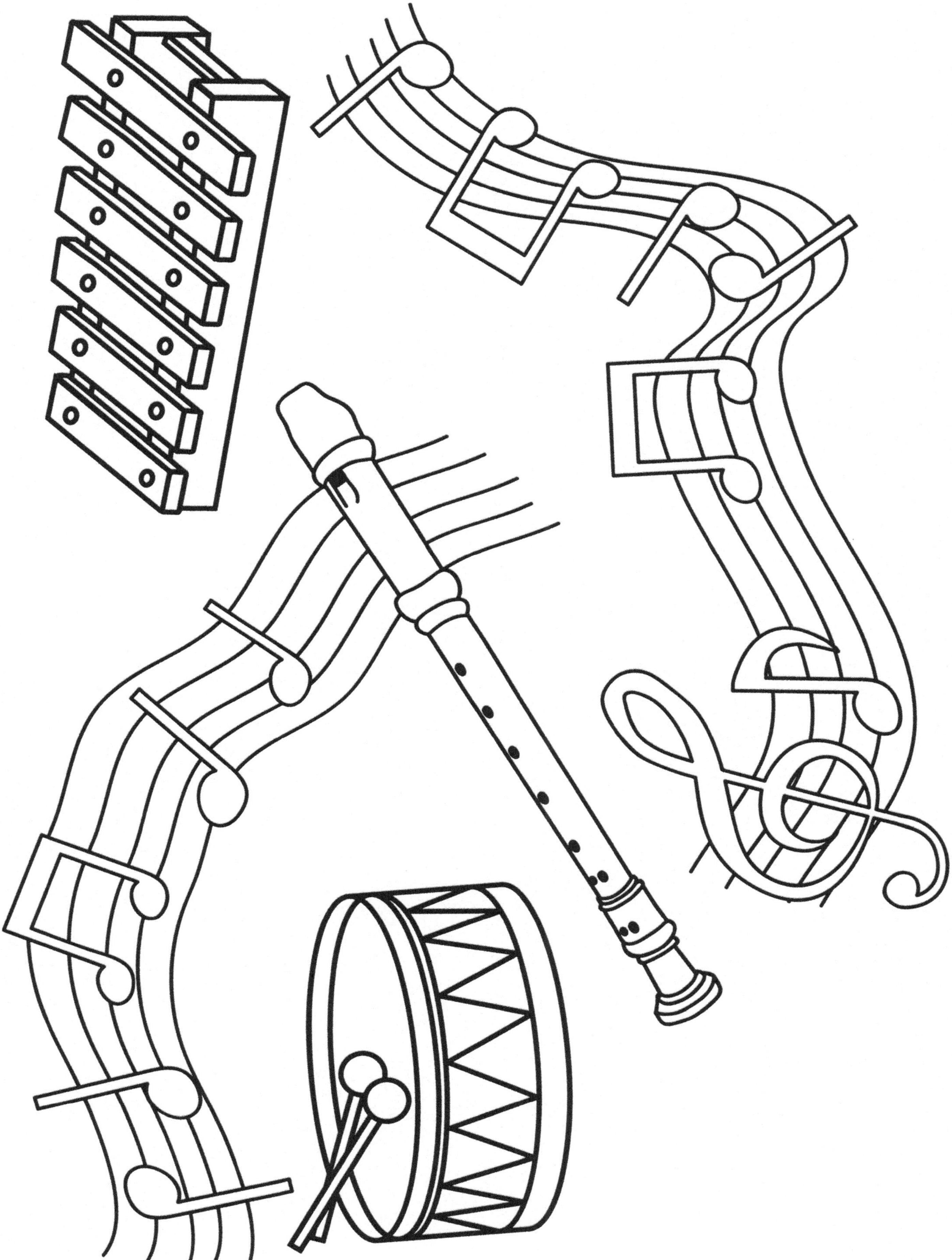

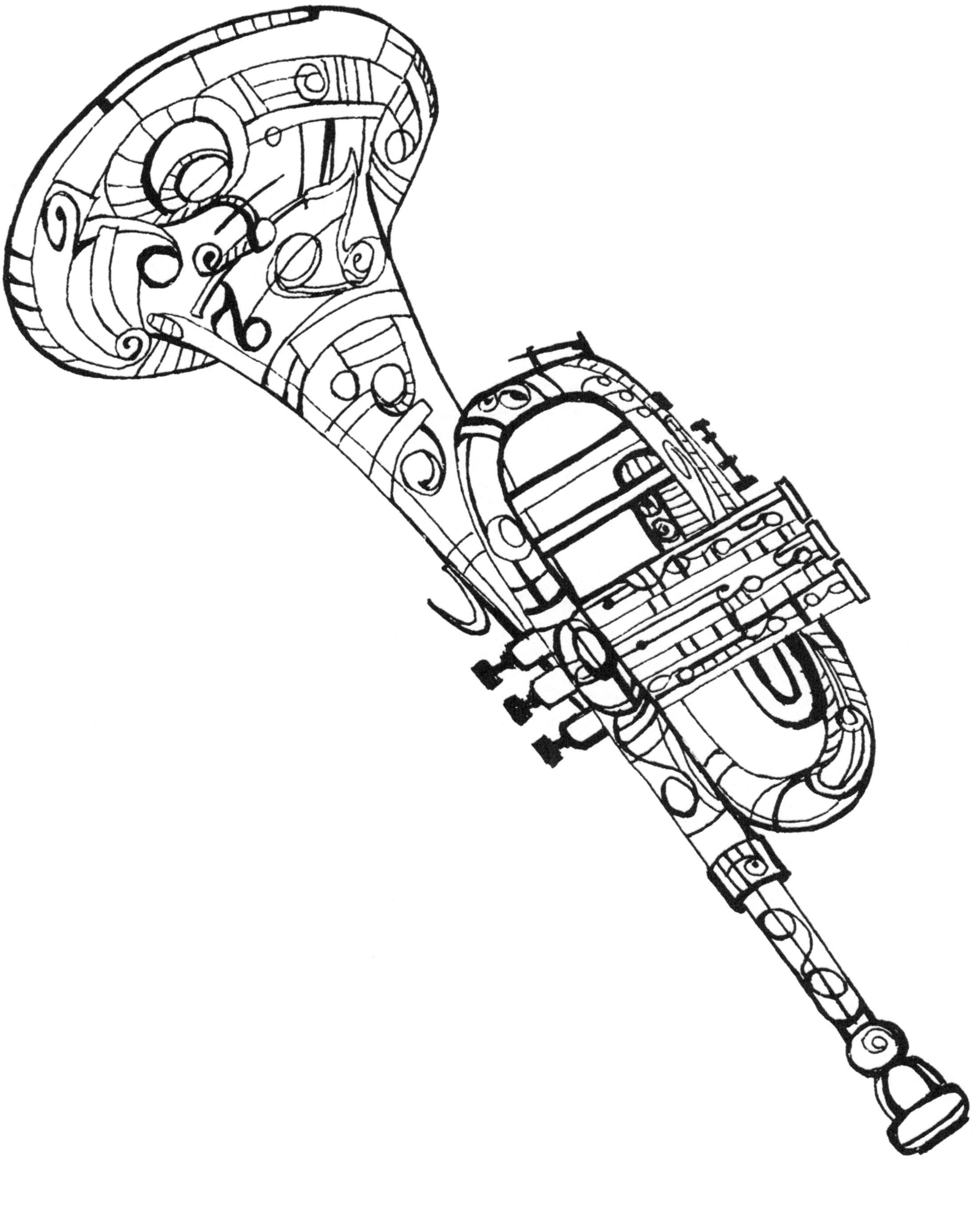

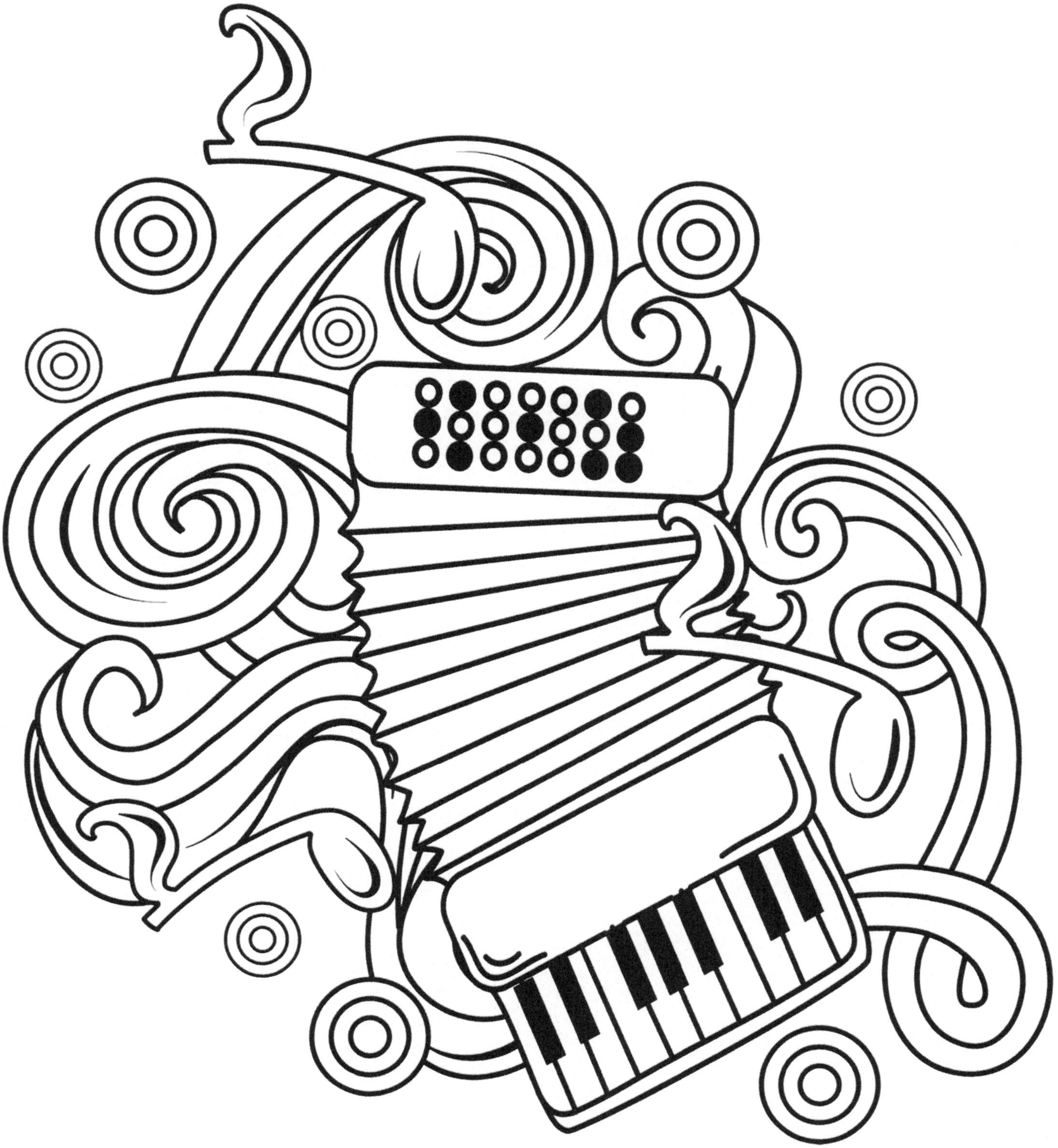

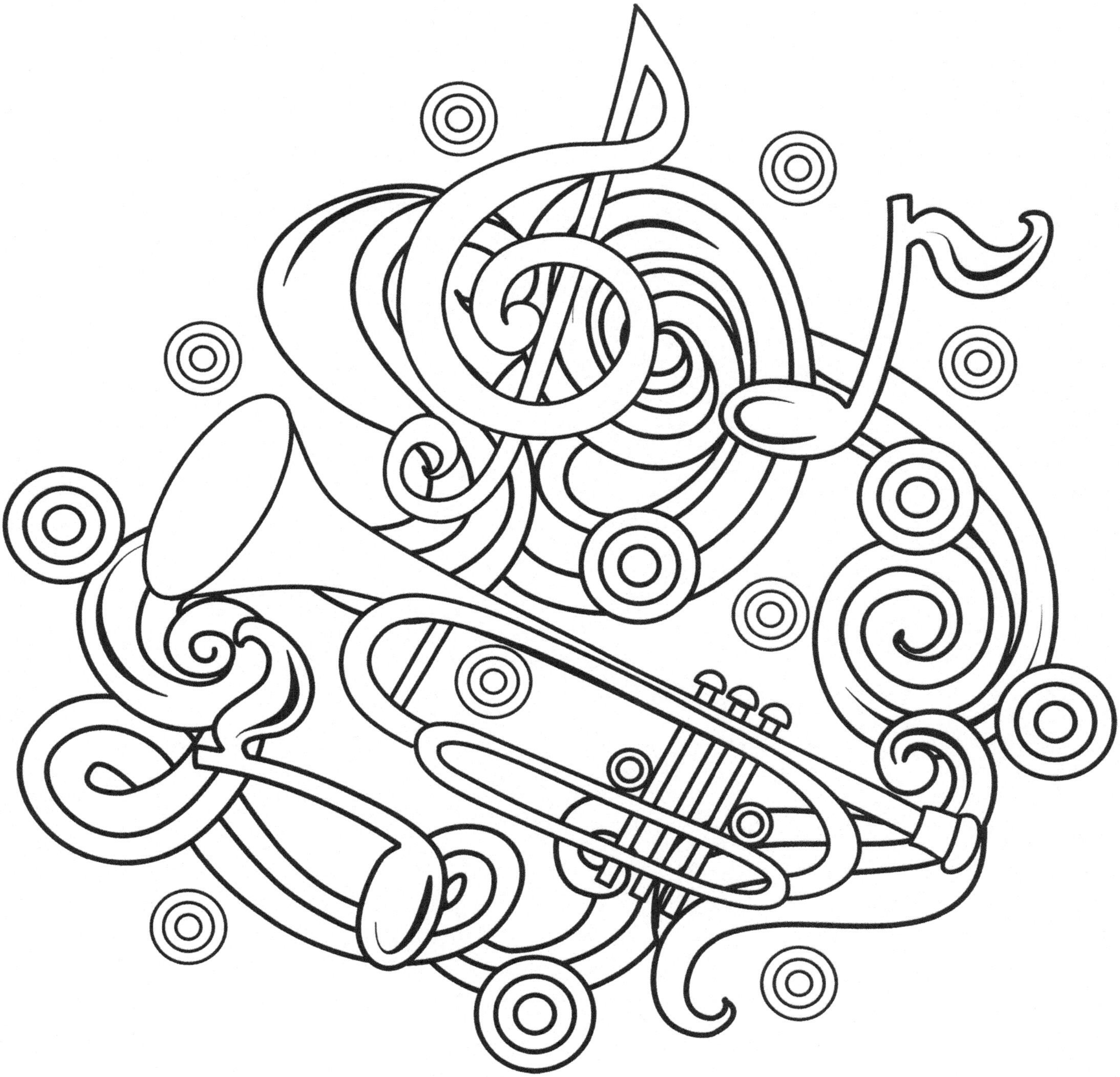

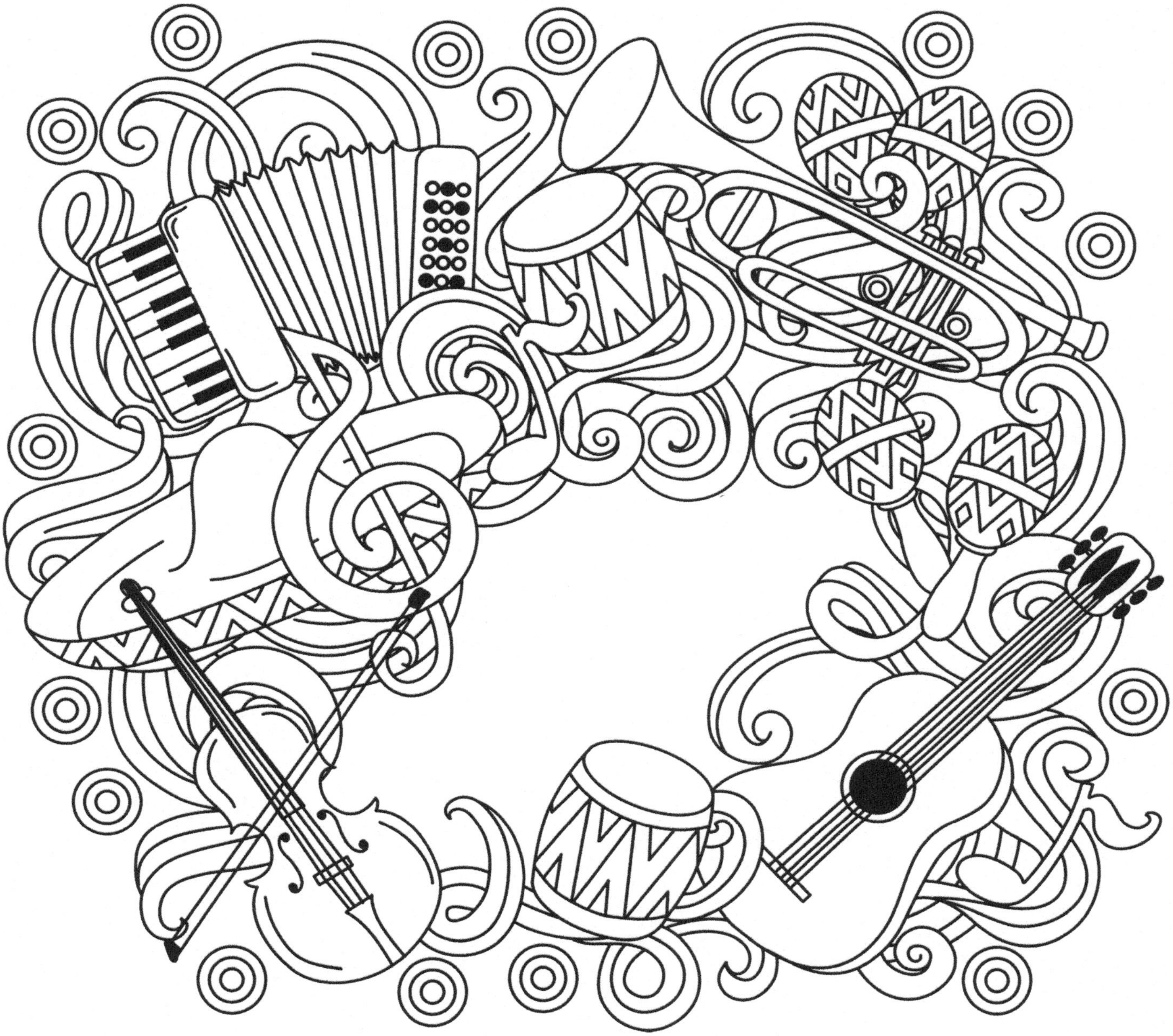

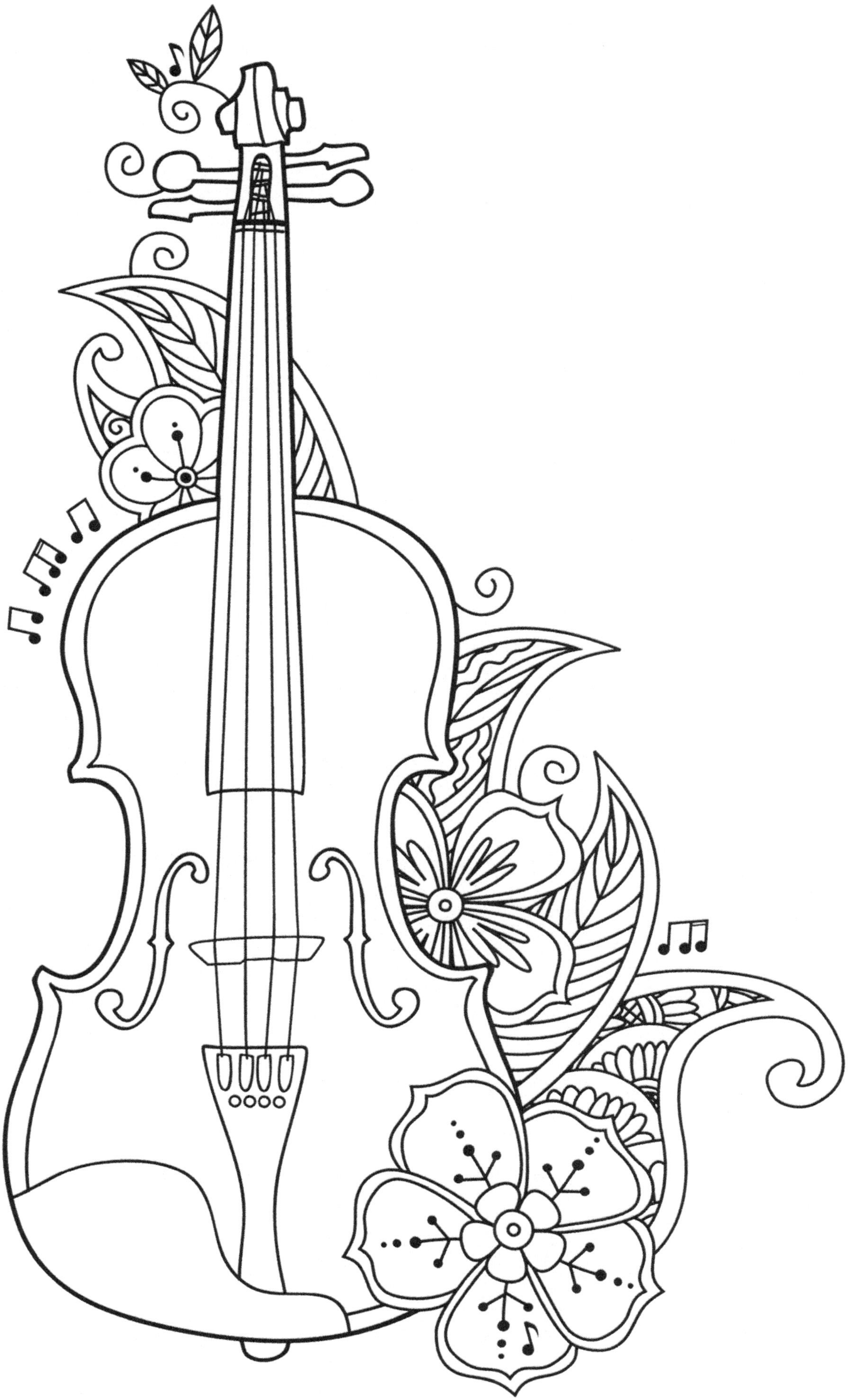

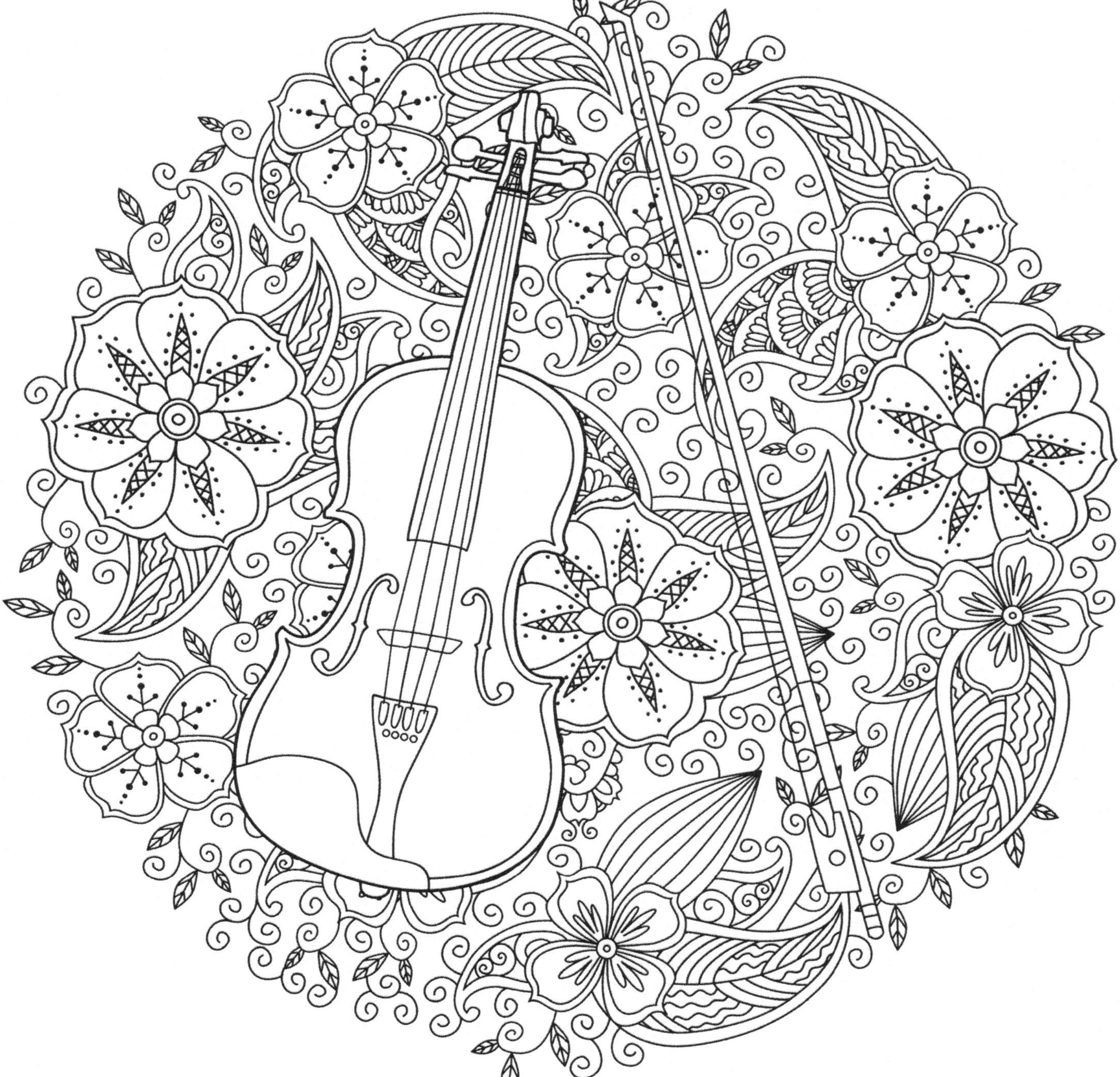

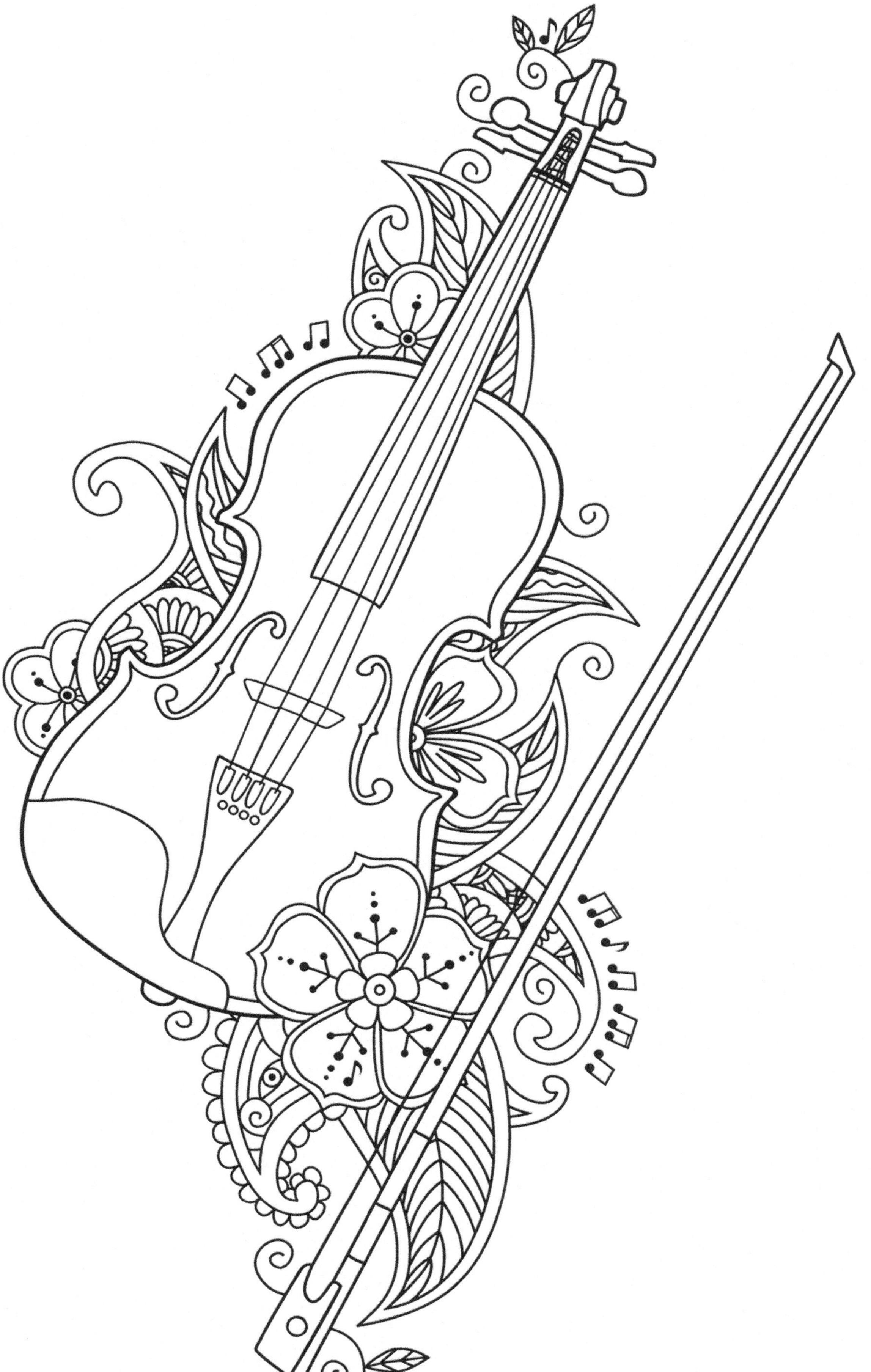

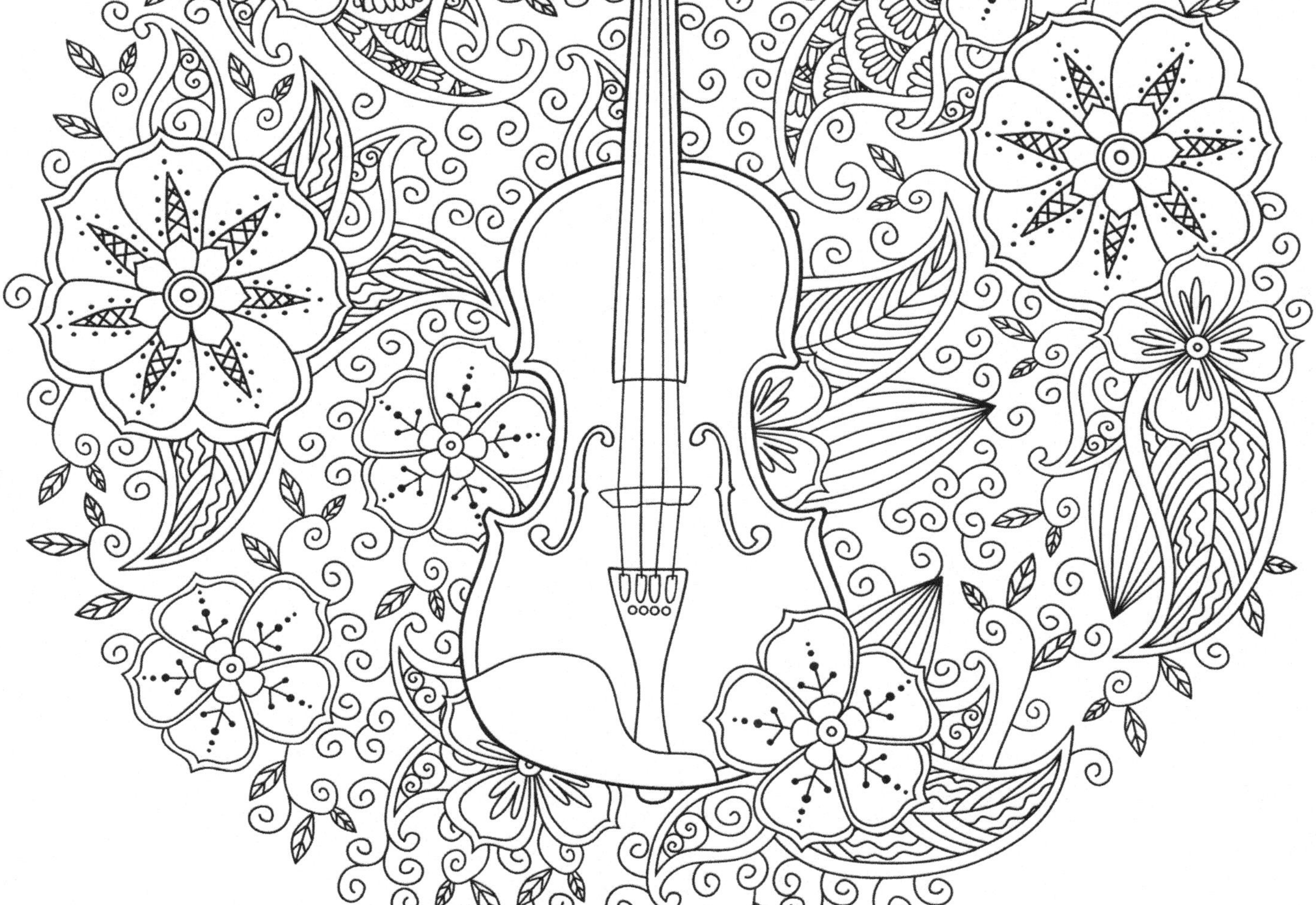

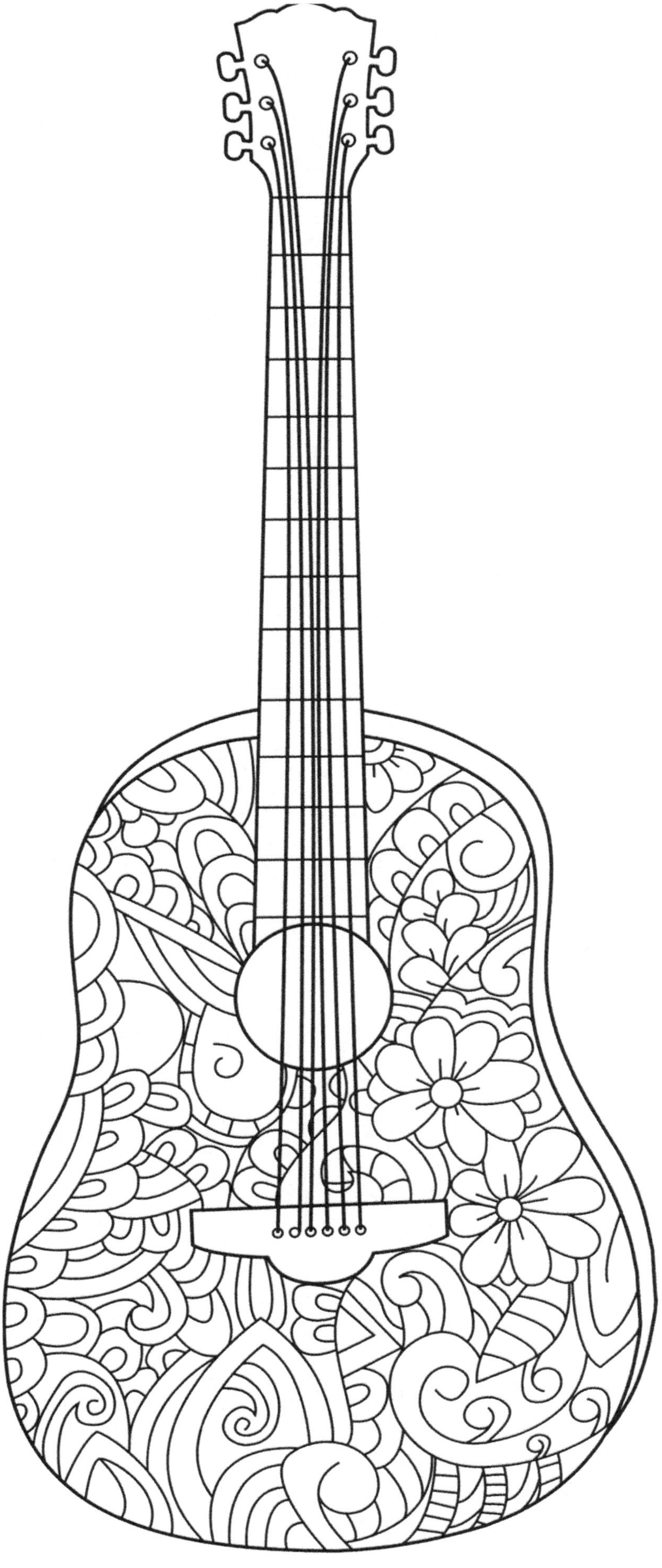

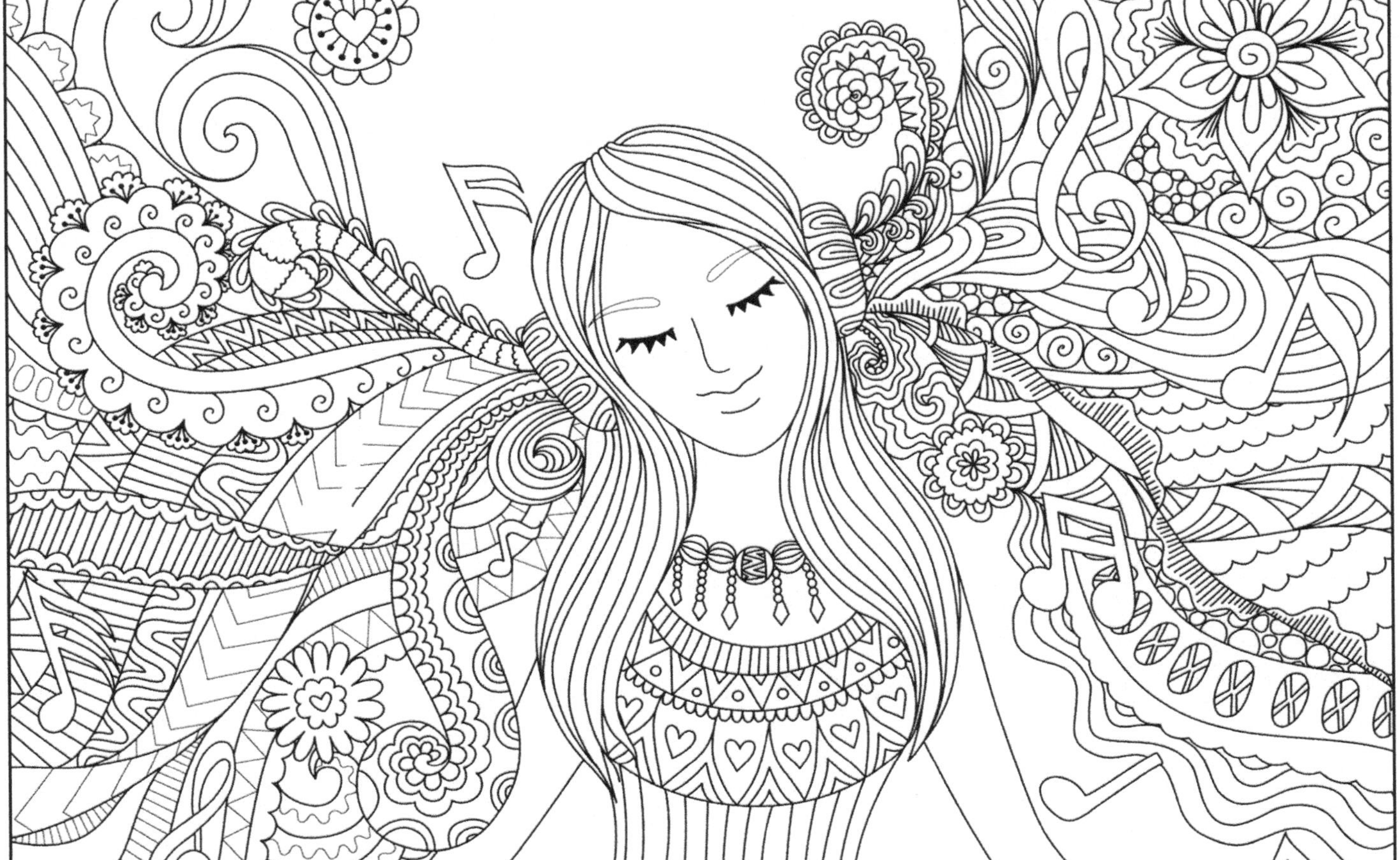

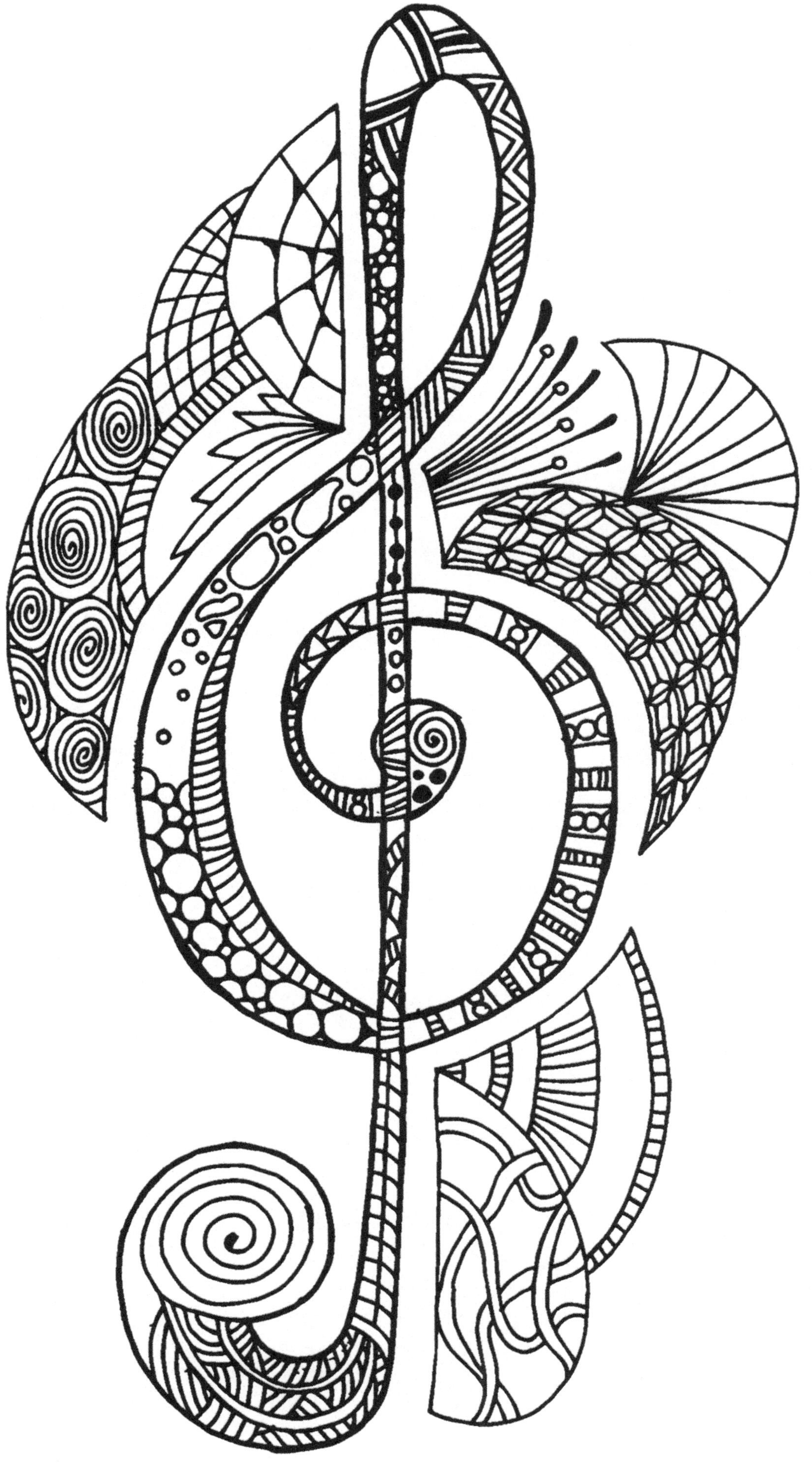

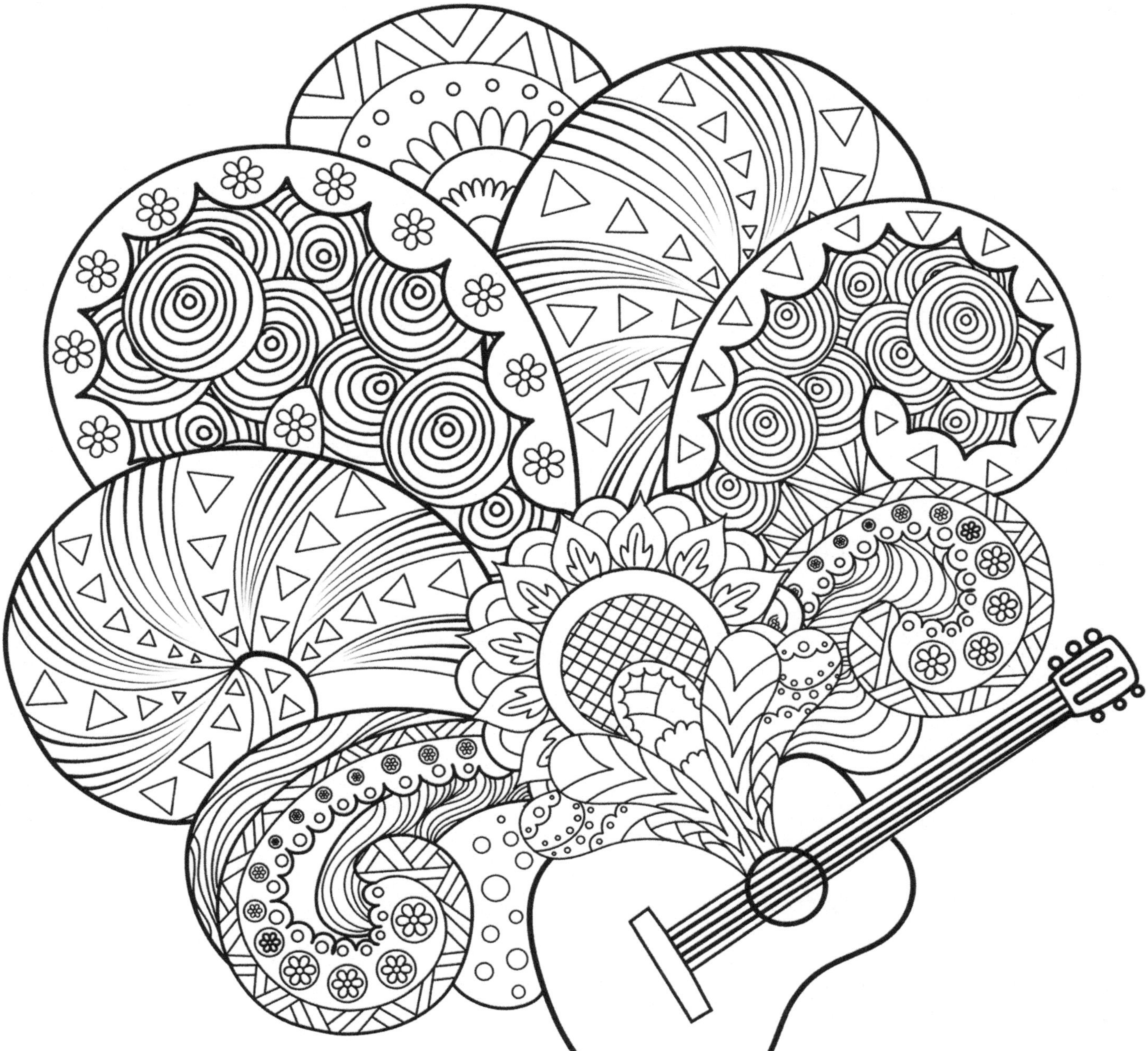

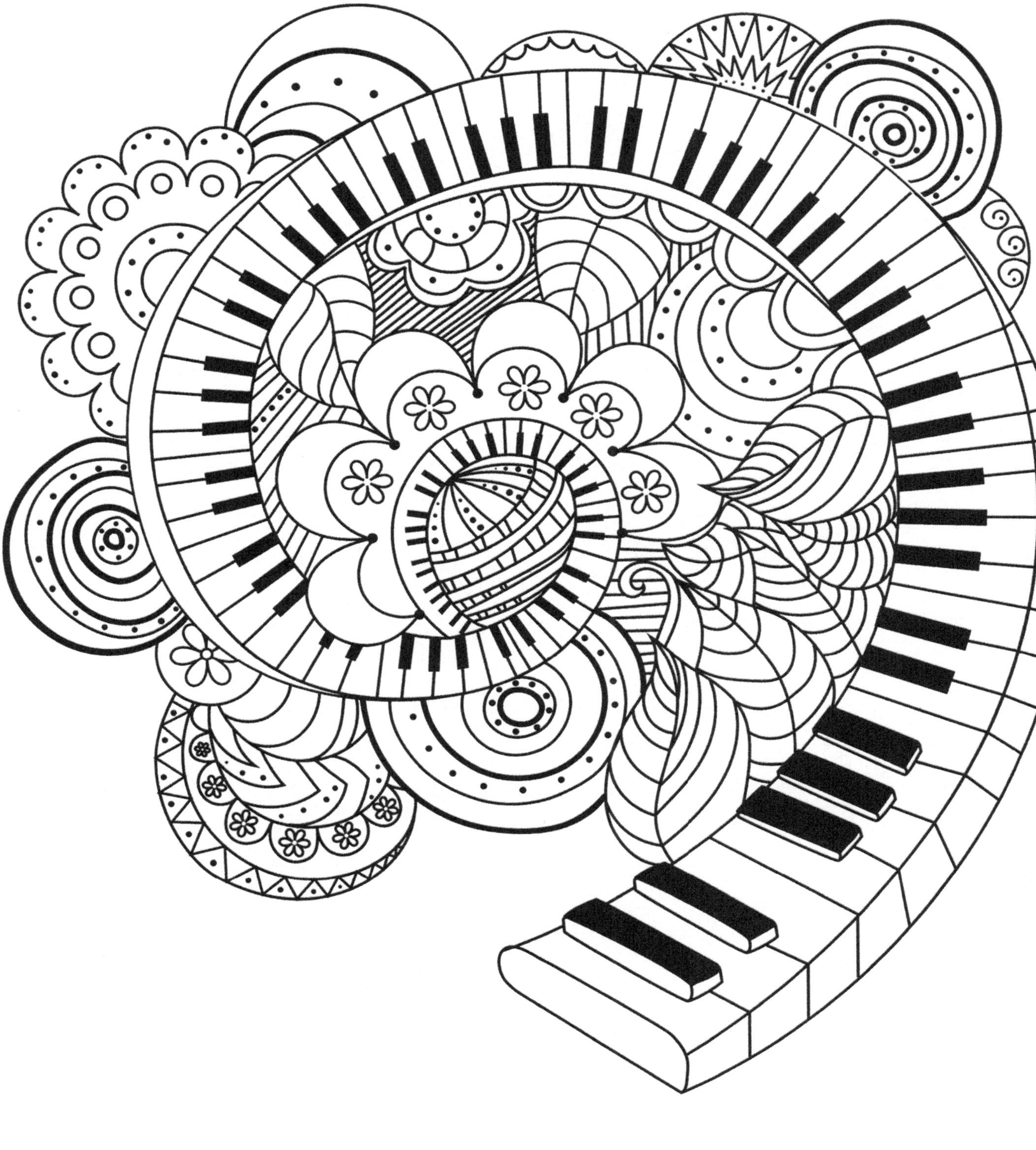

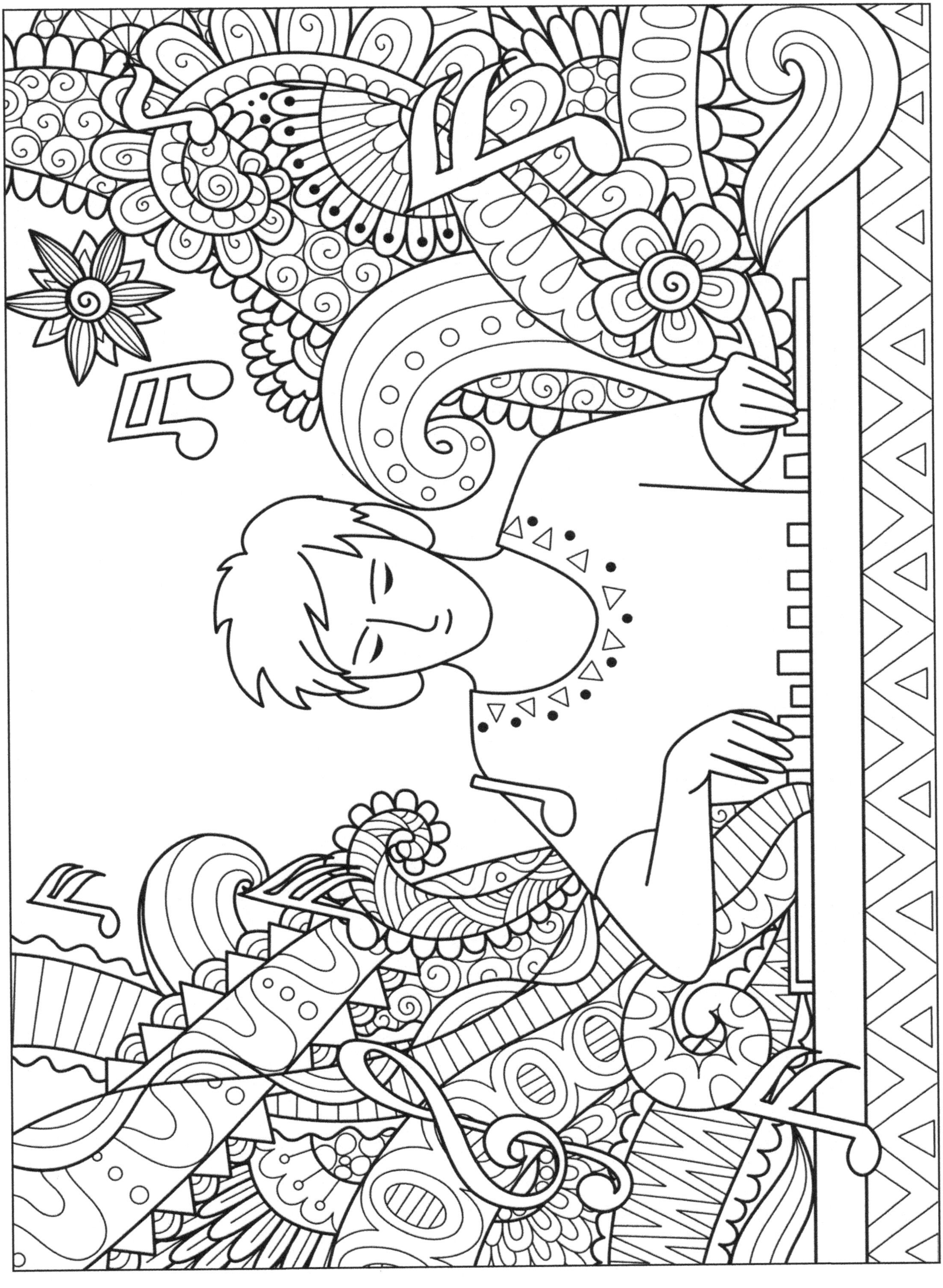

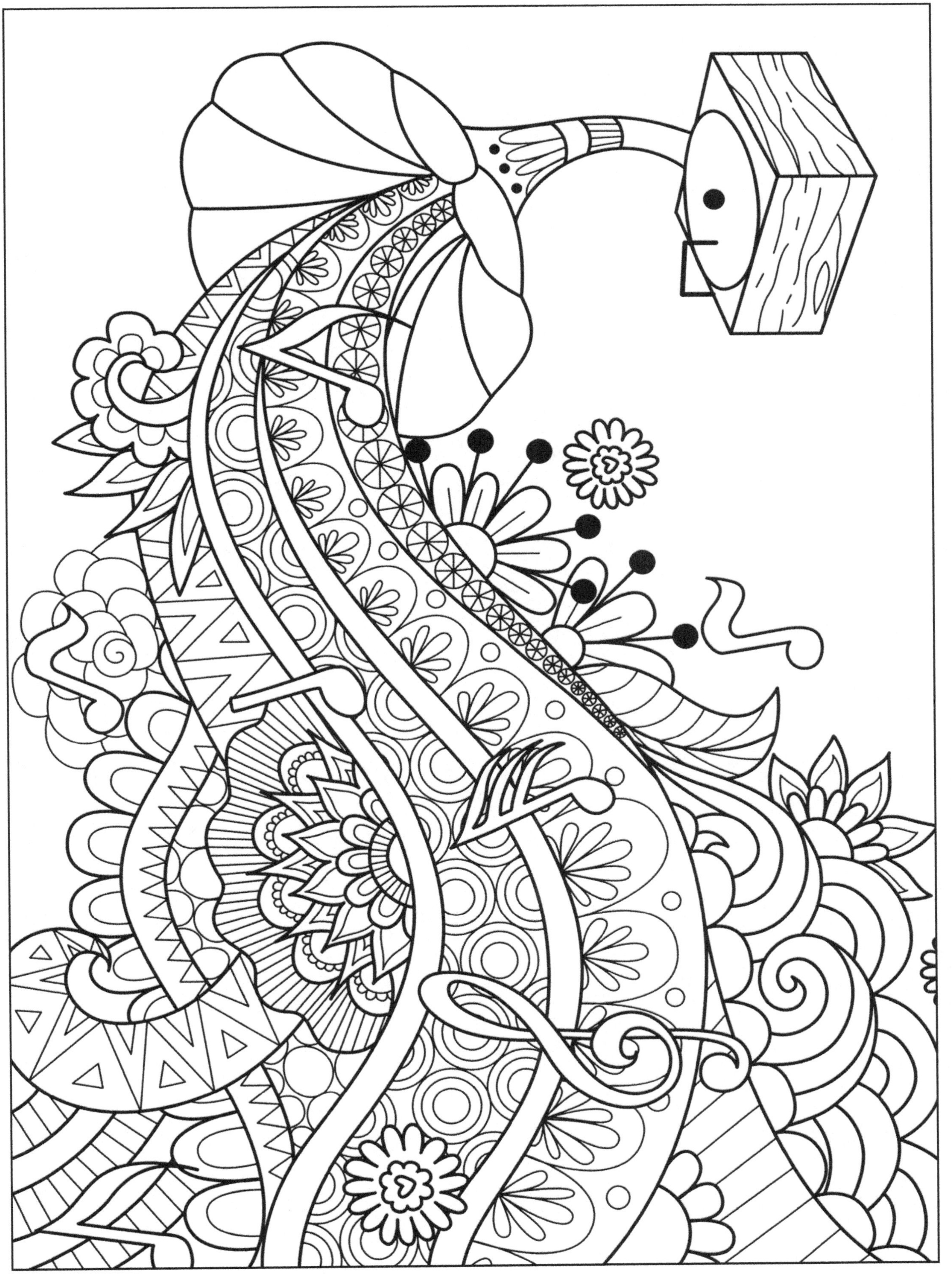

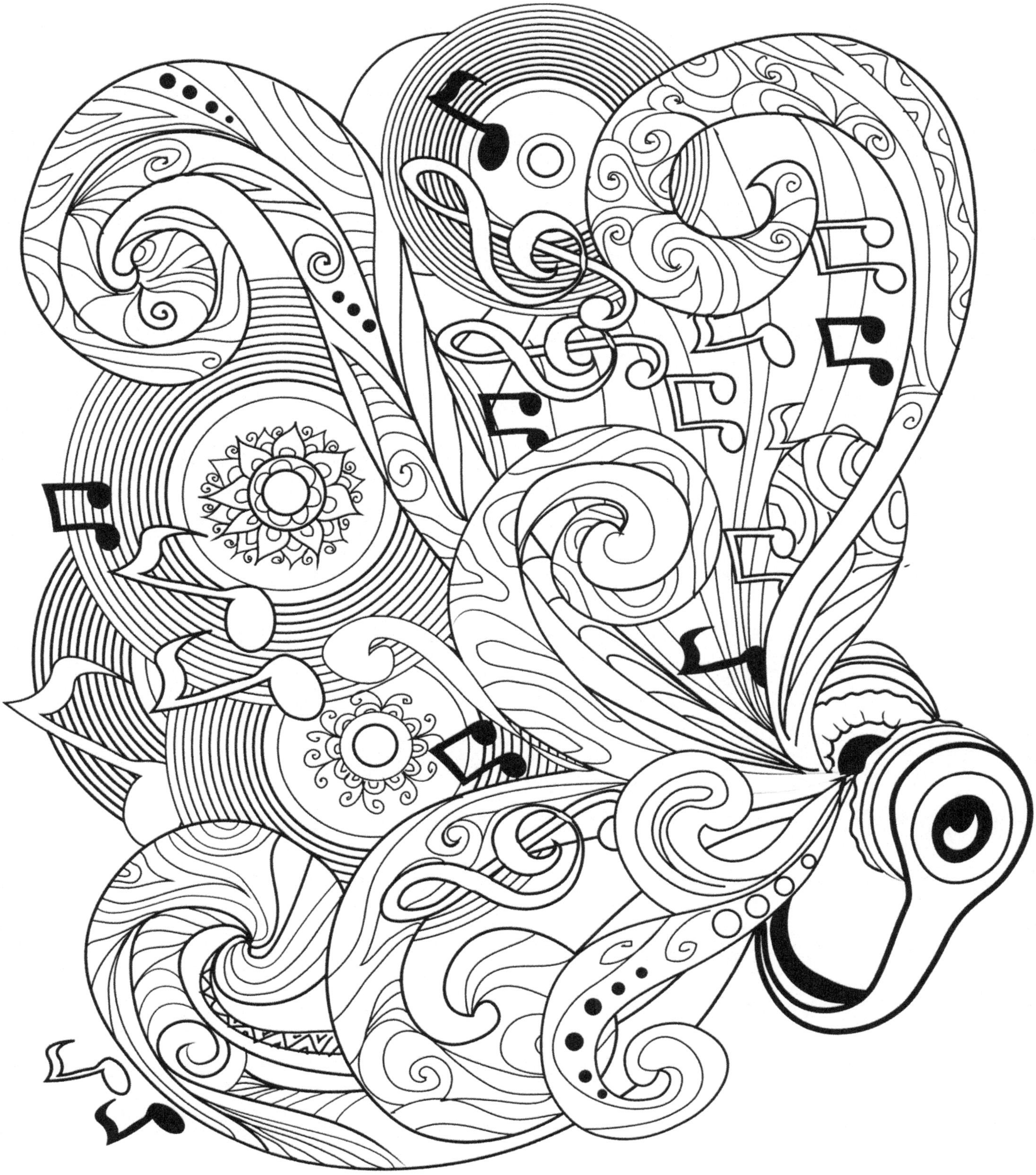

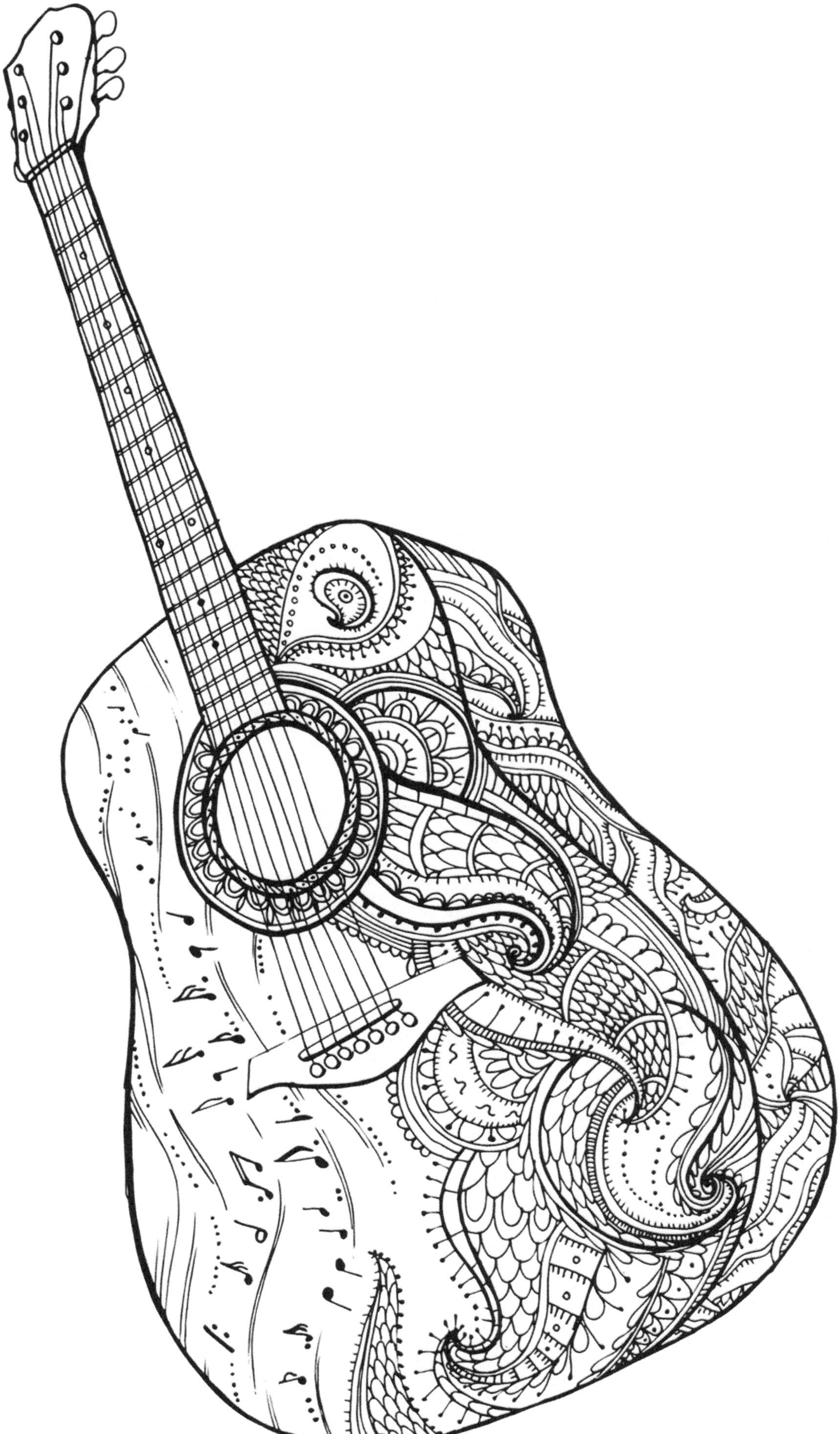

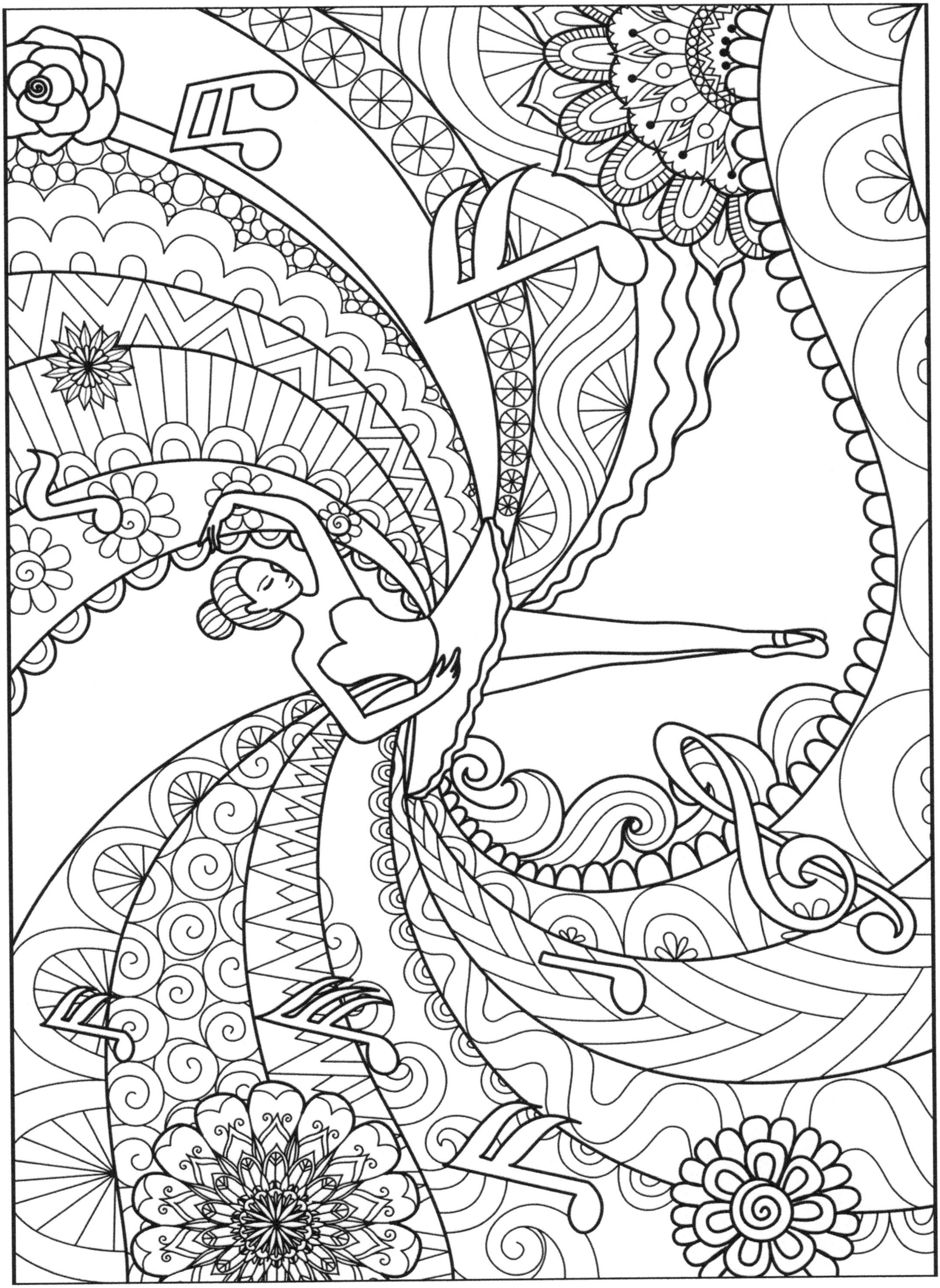

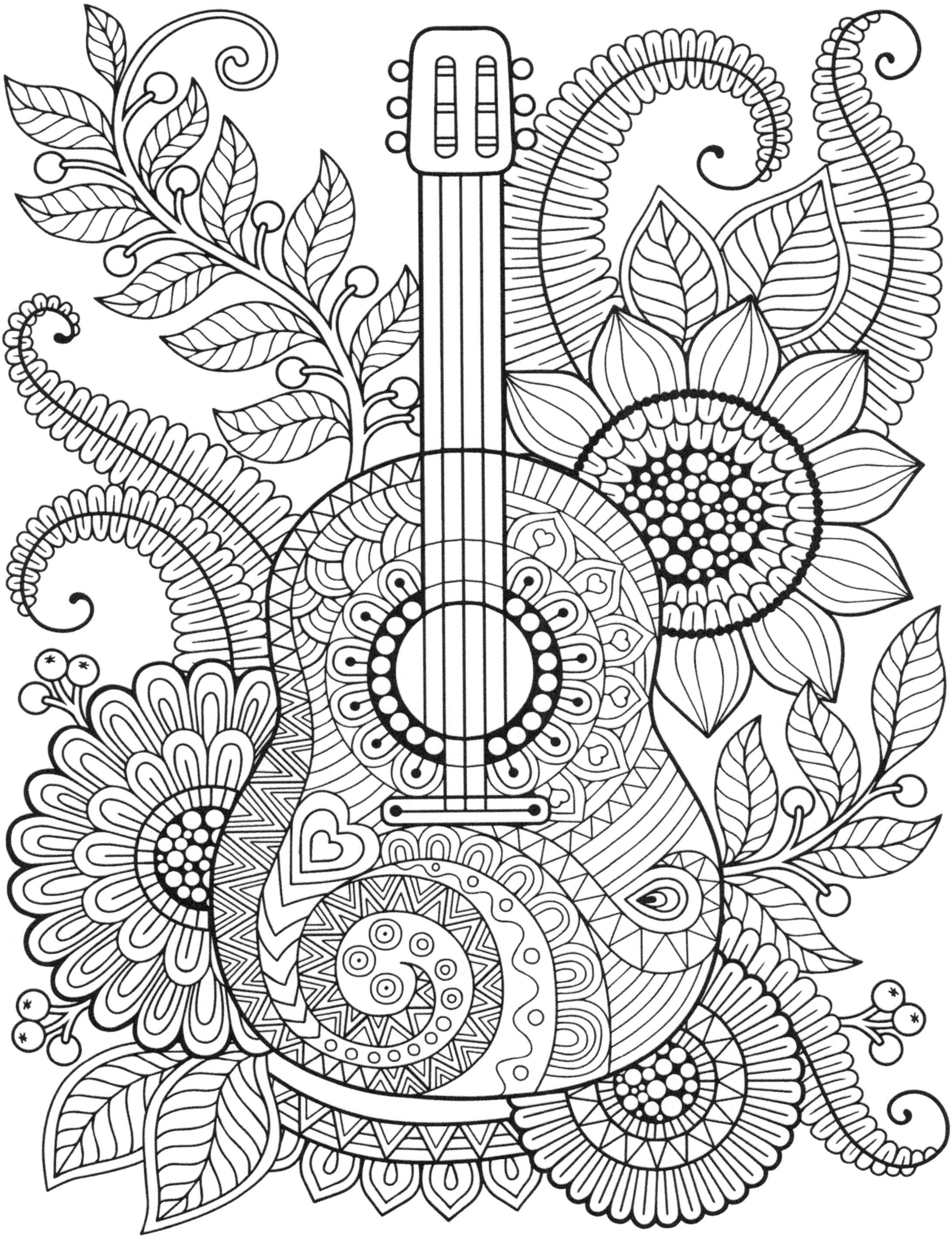

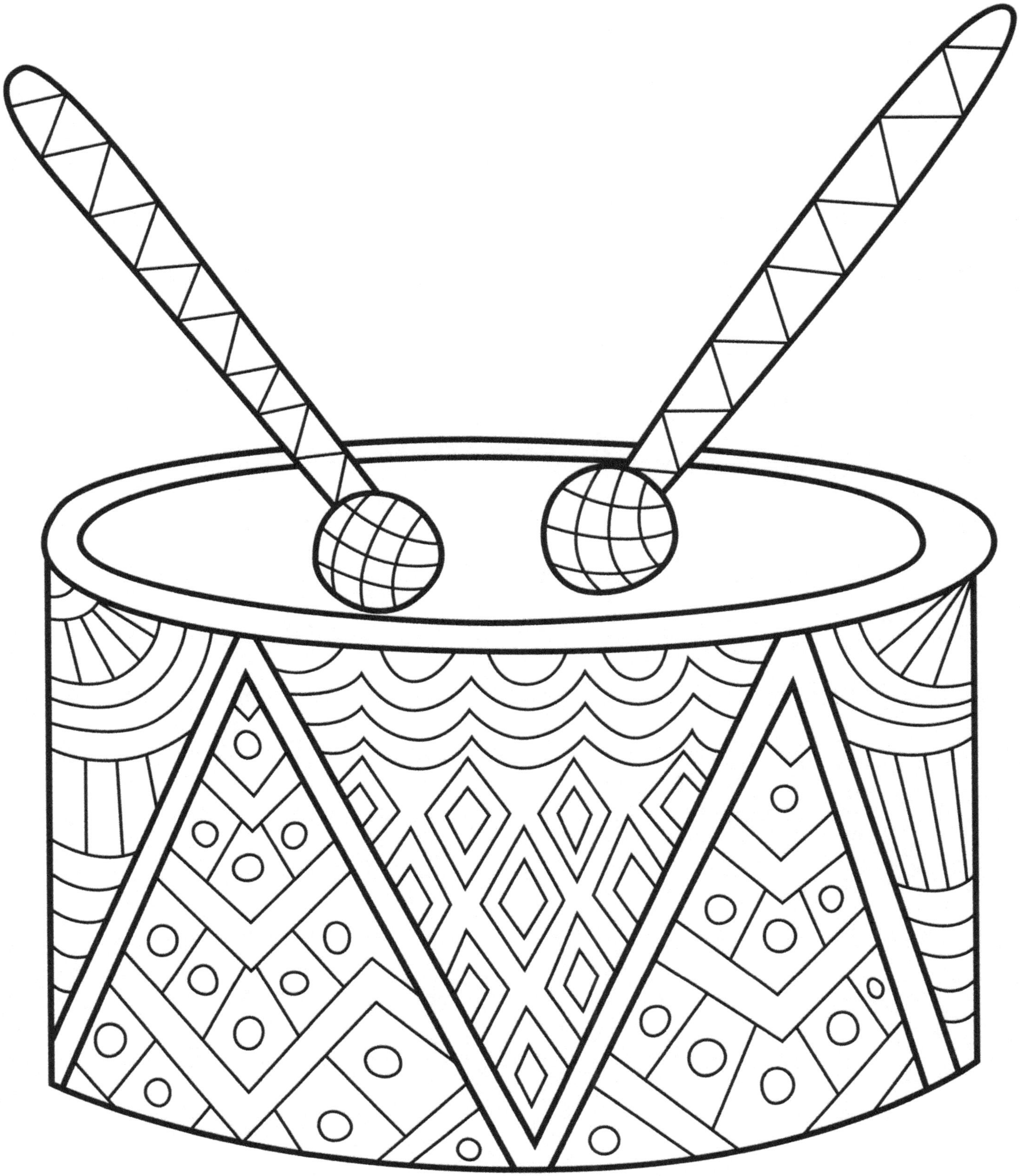

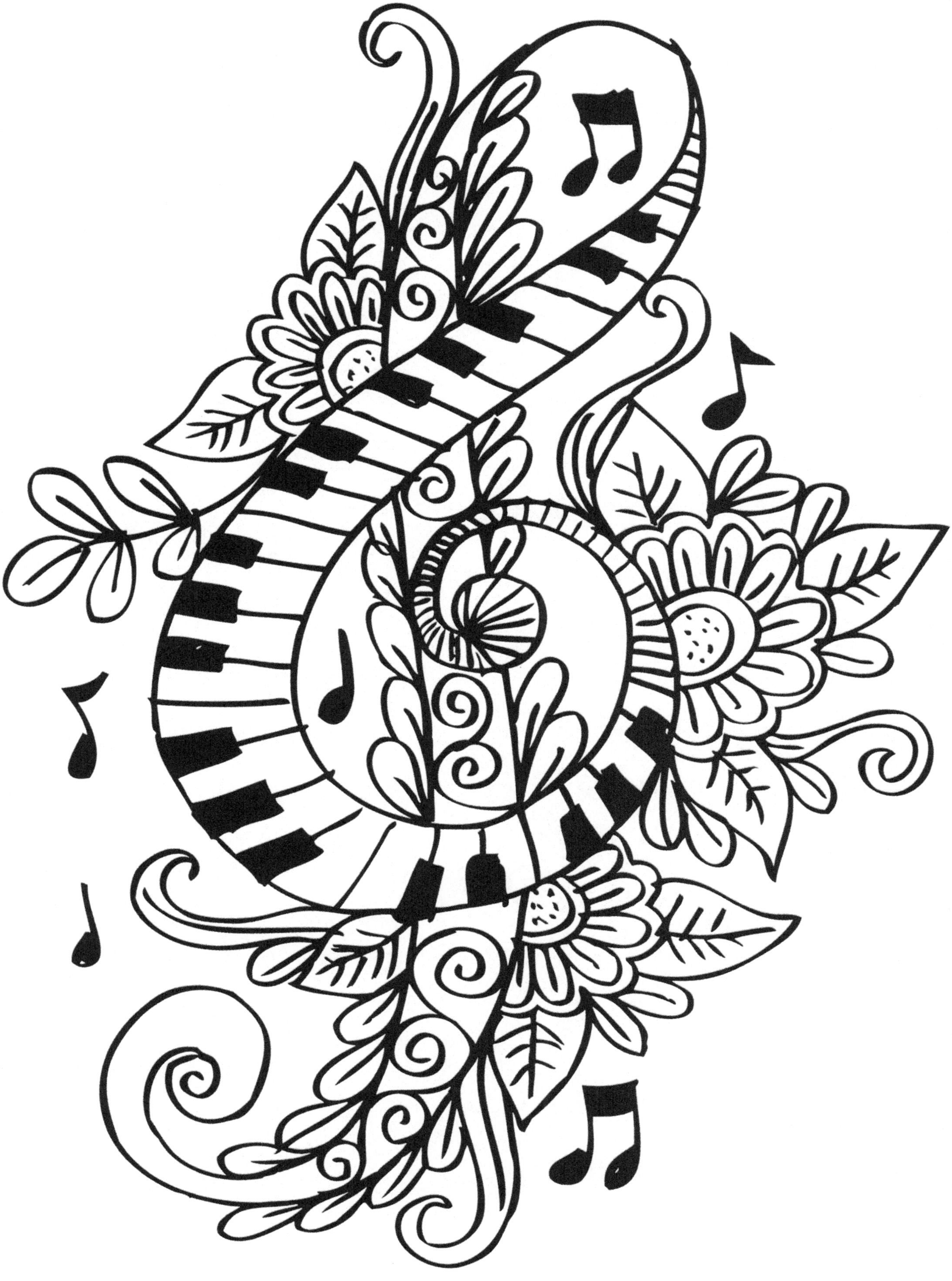

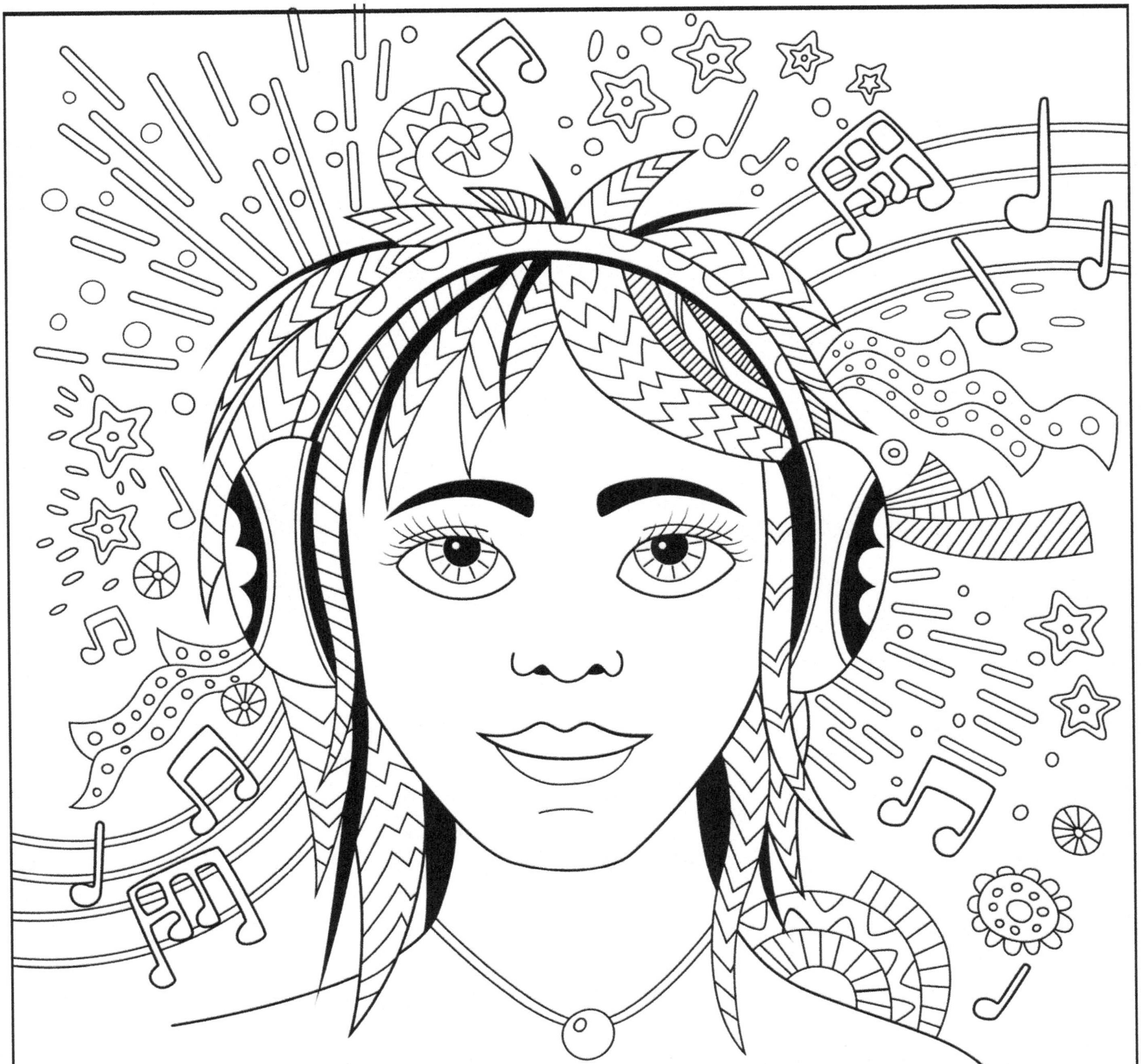

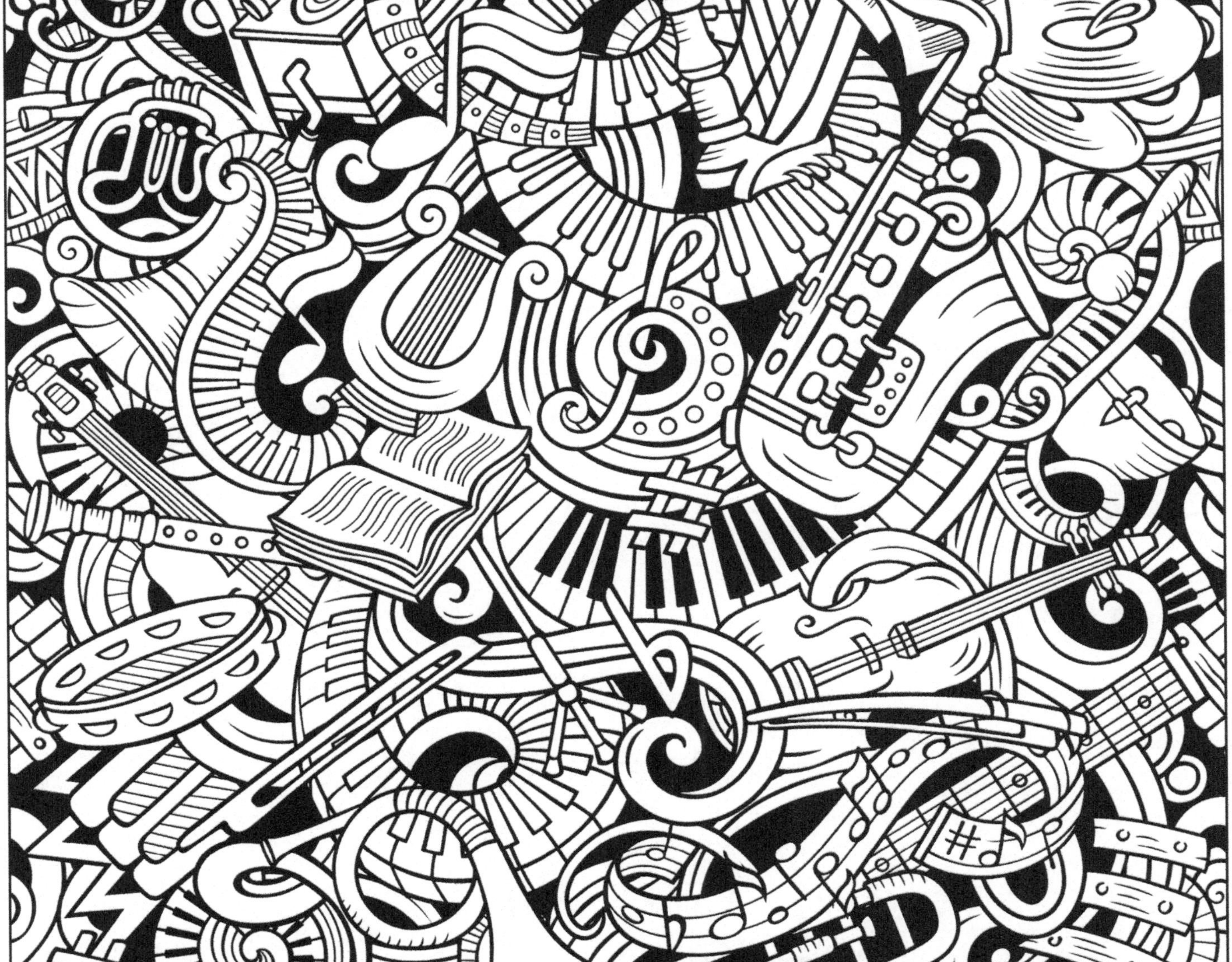

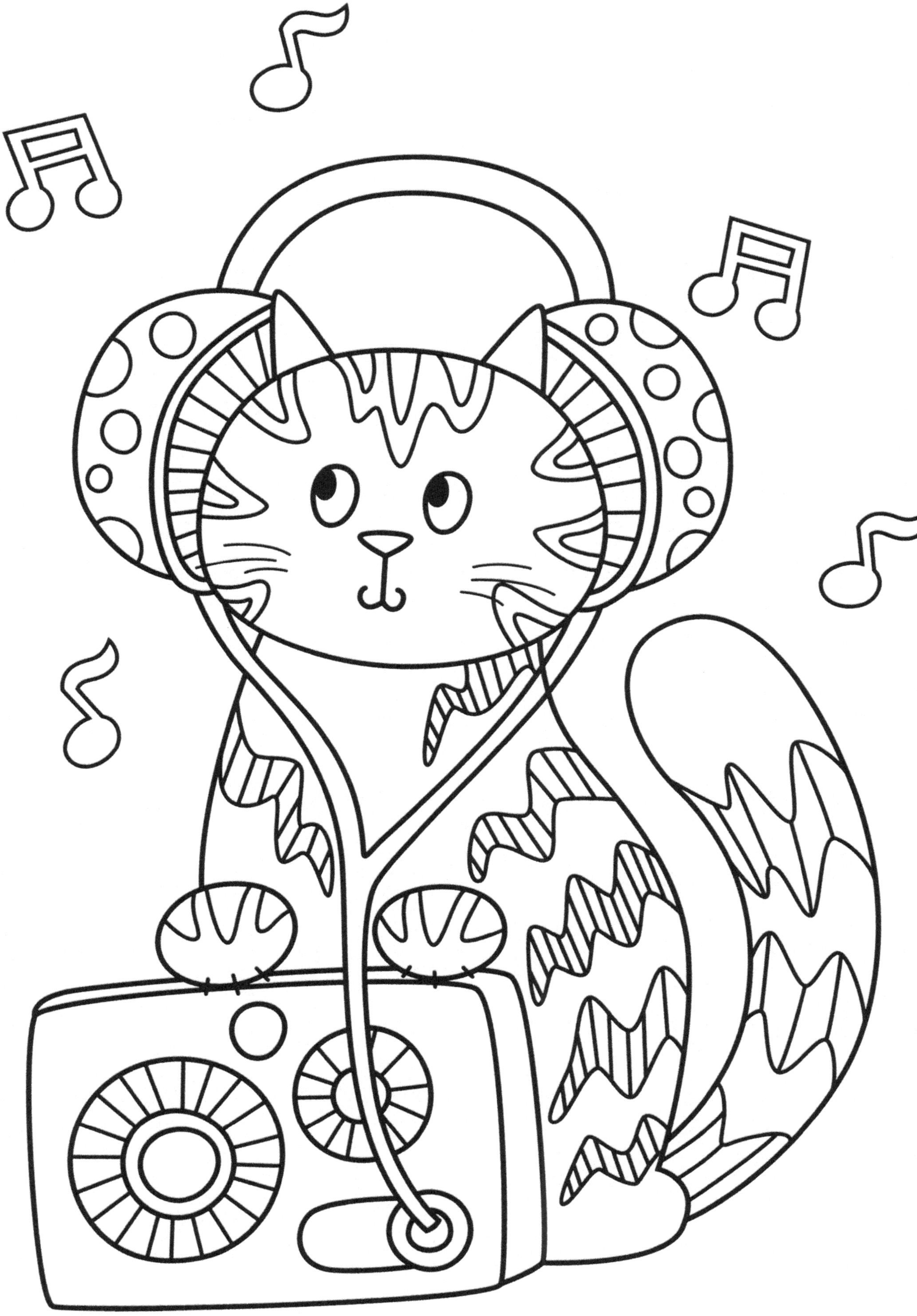

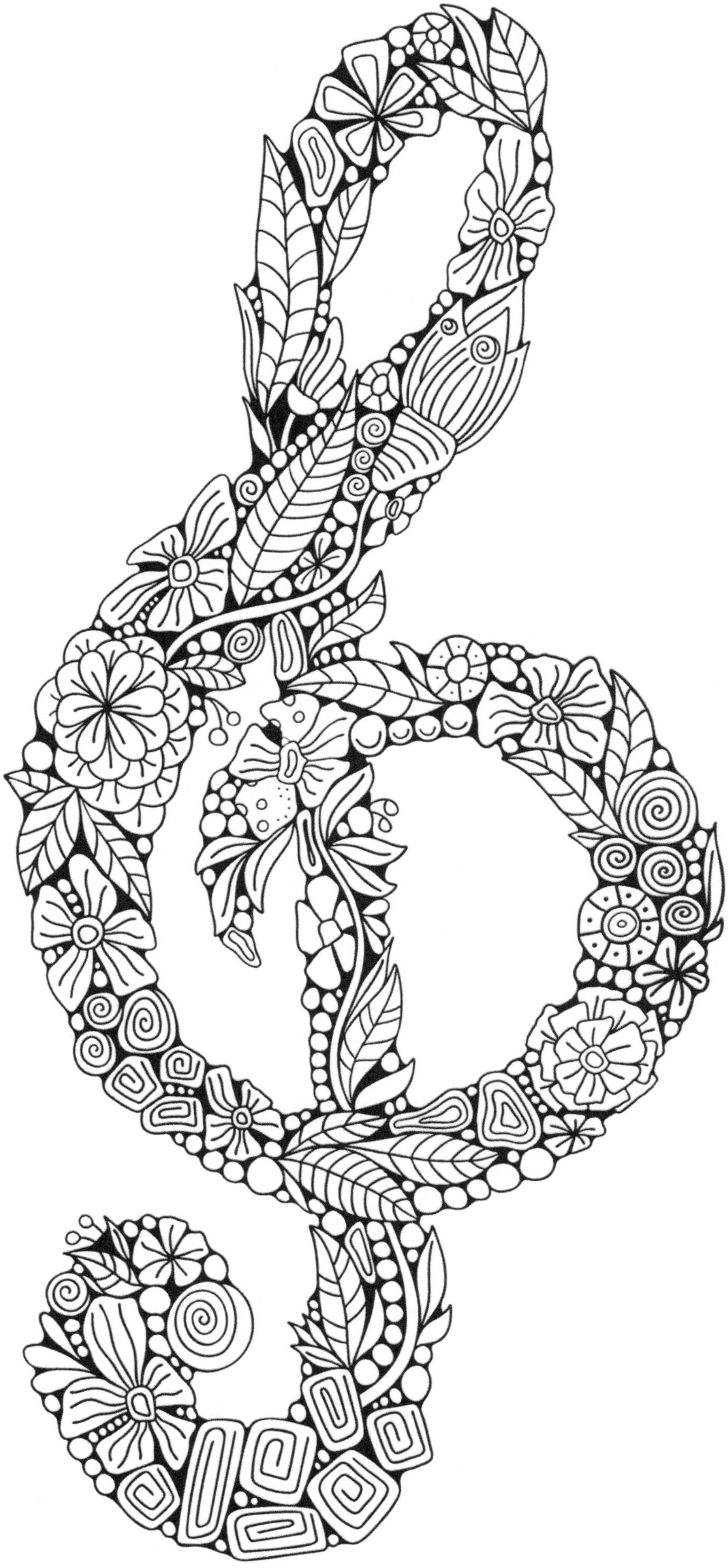

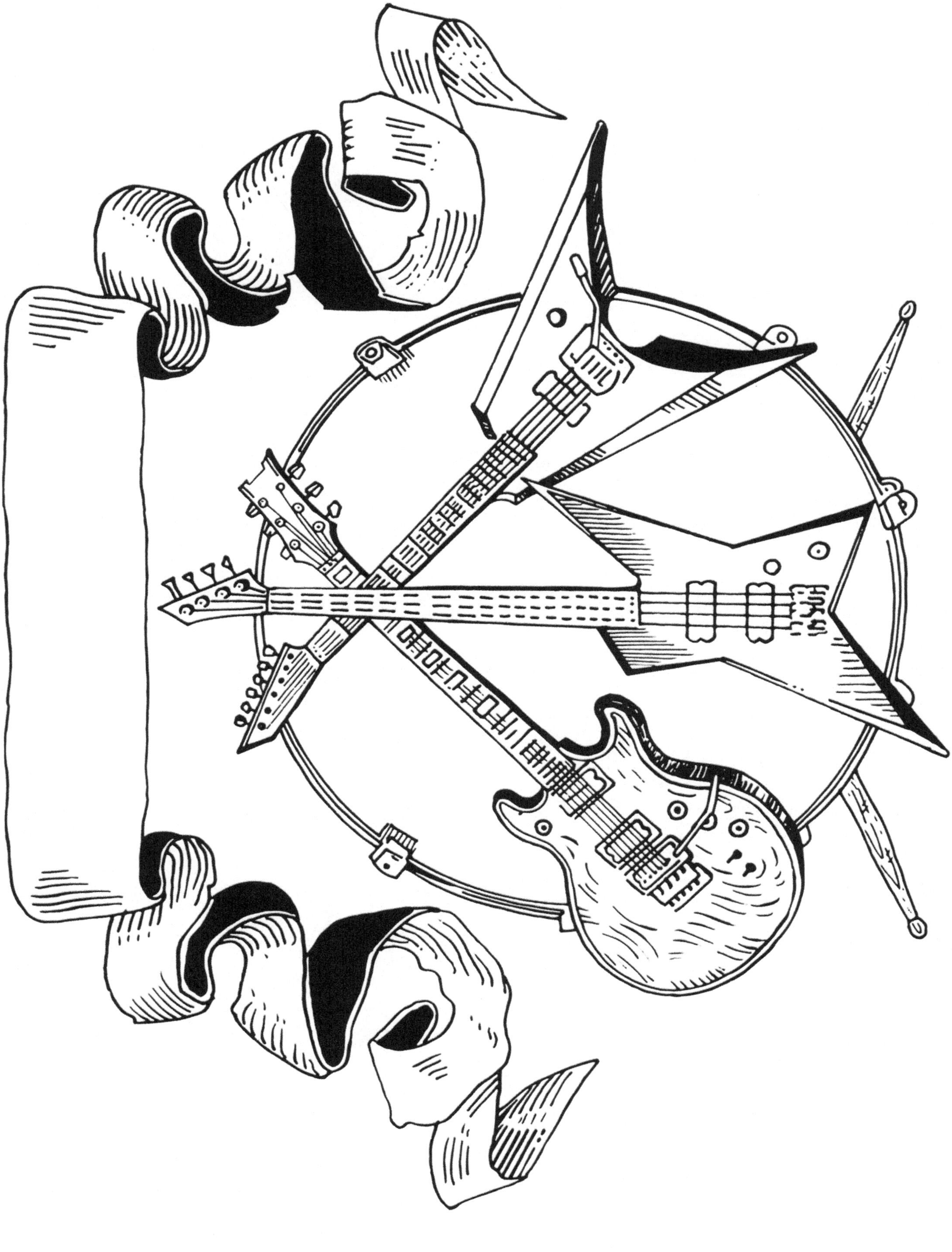

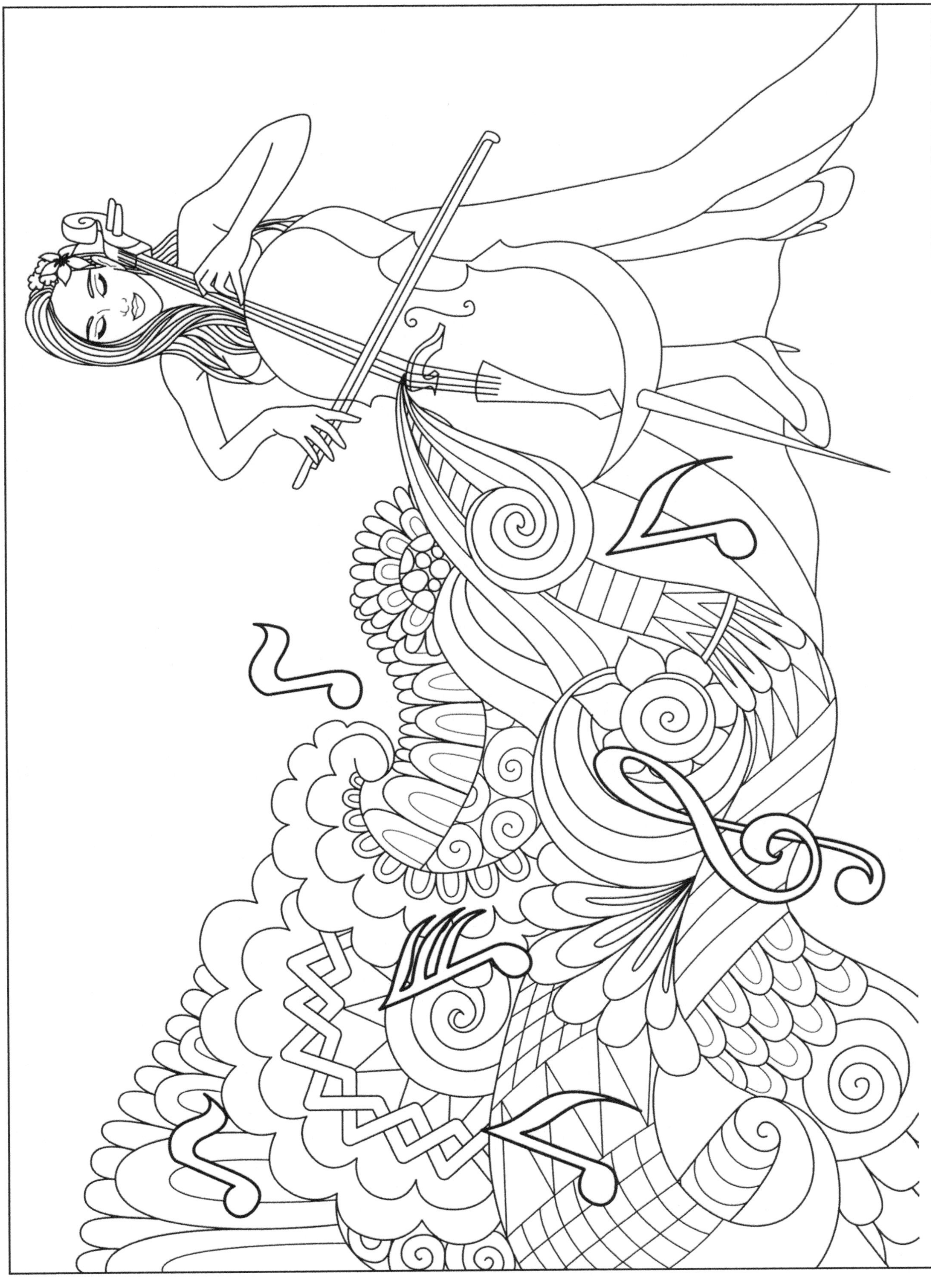

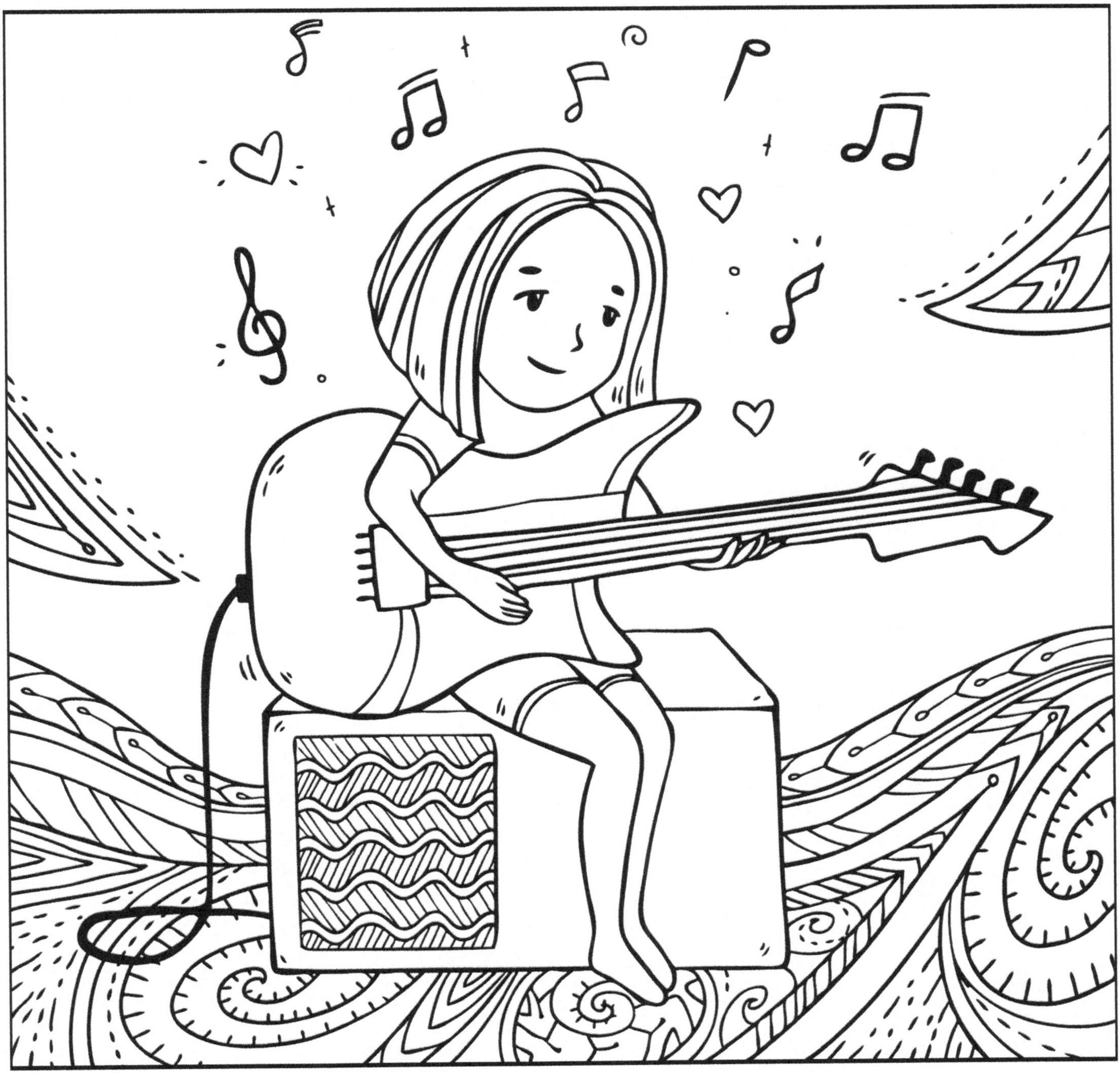

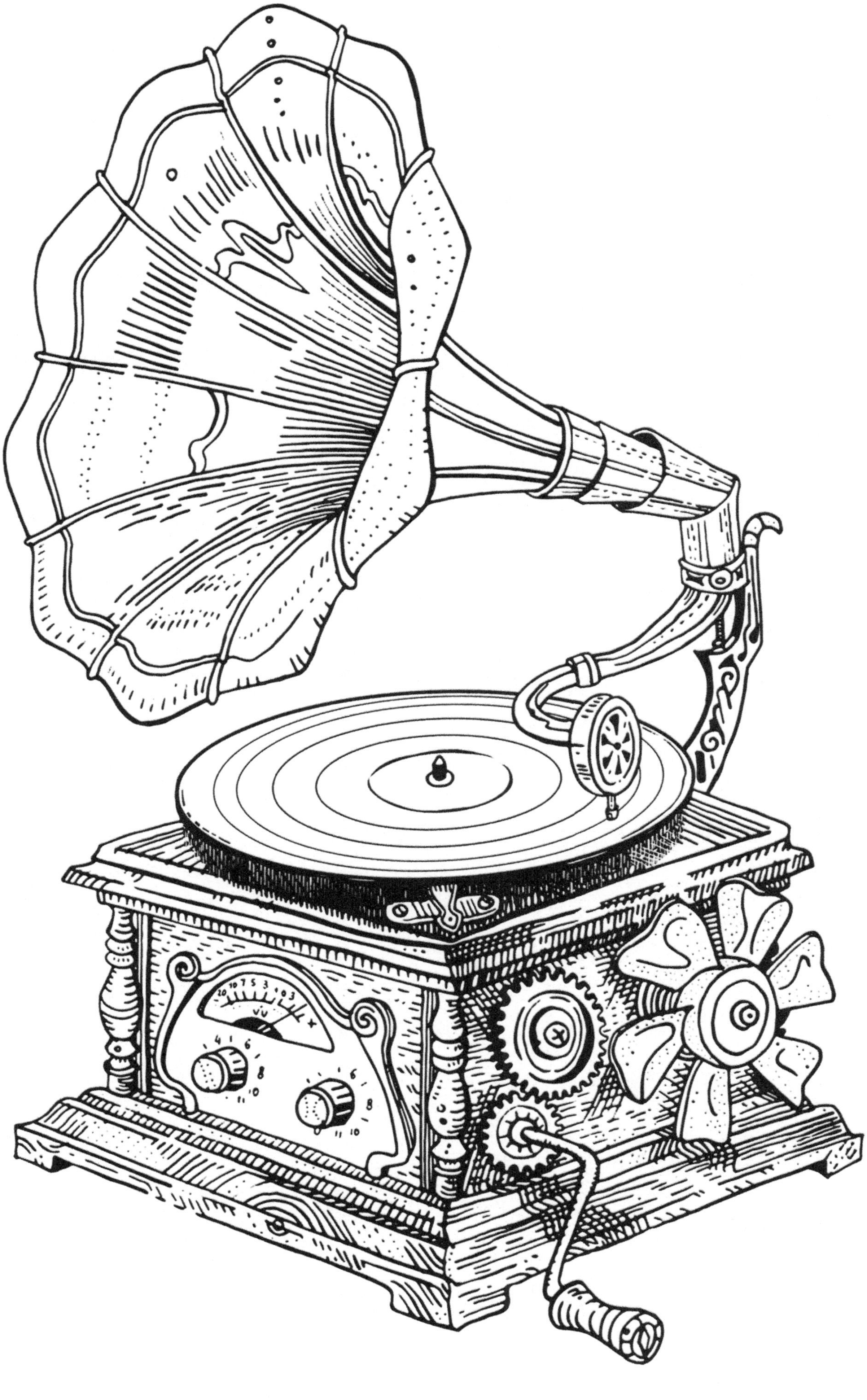
20 10 7 5 3 1 0 3
VU
+
4 6 8 10 11
6 8 10 11

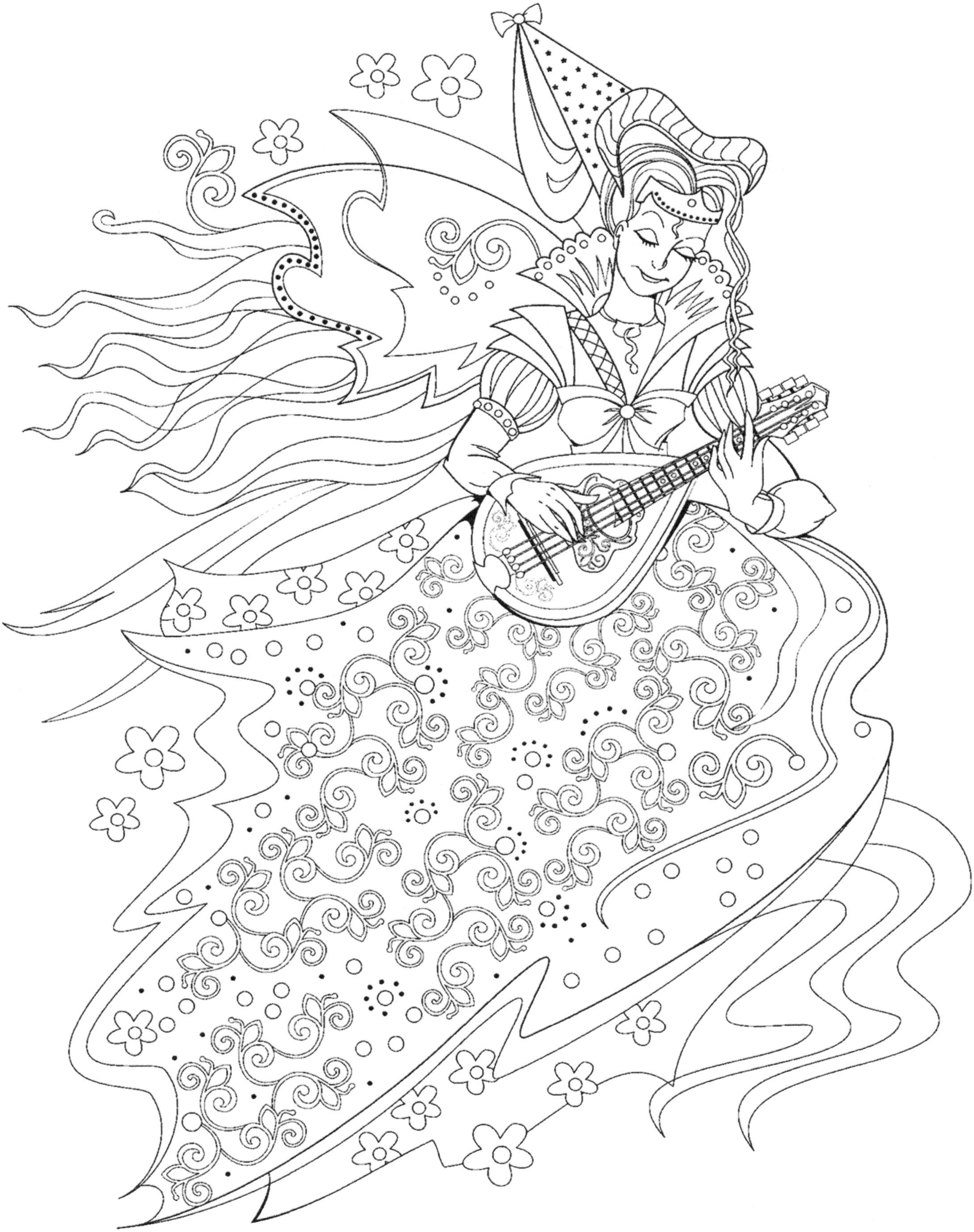

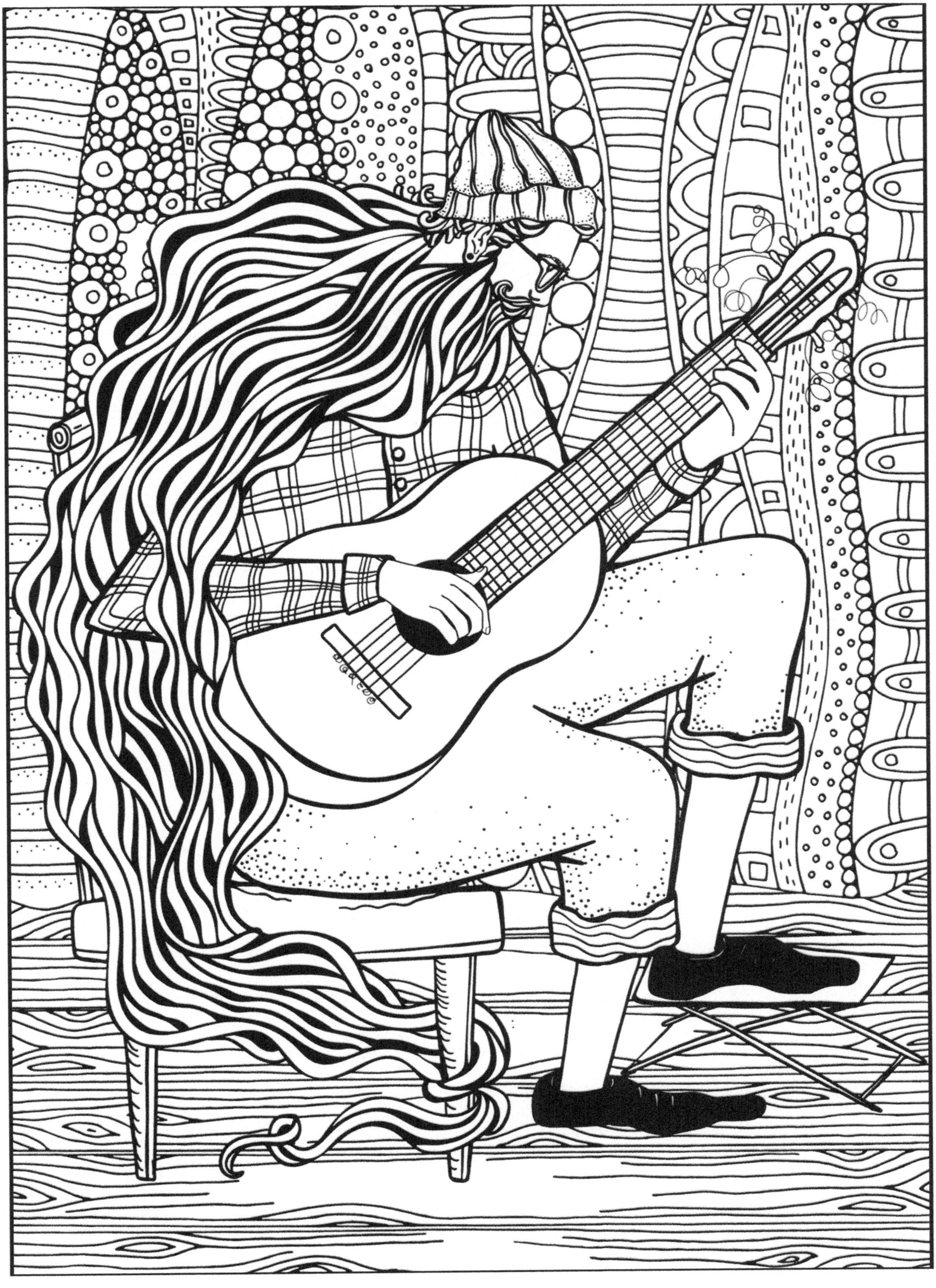

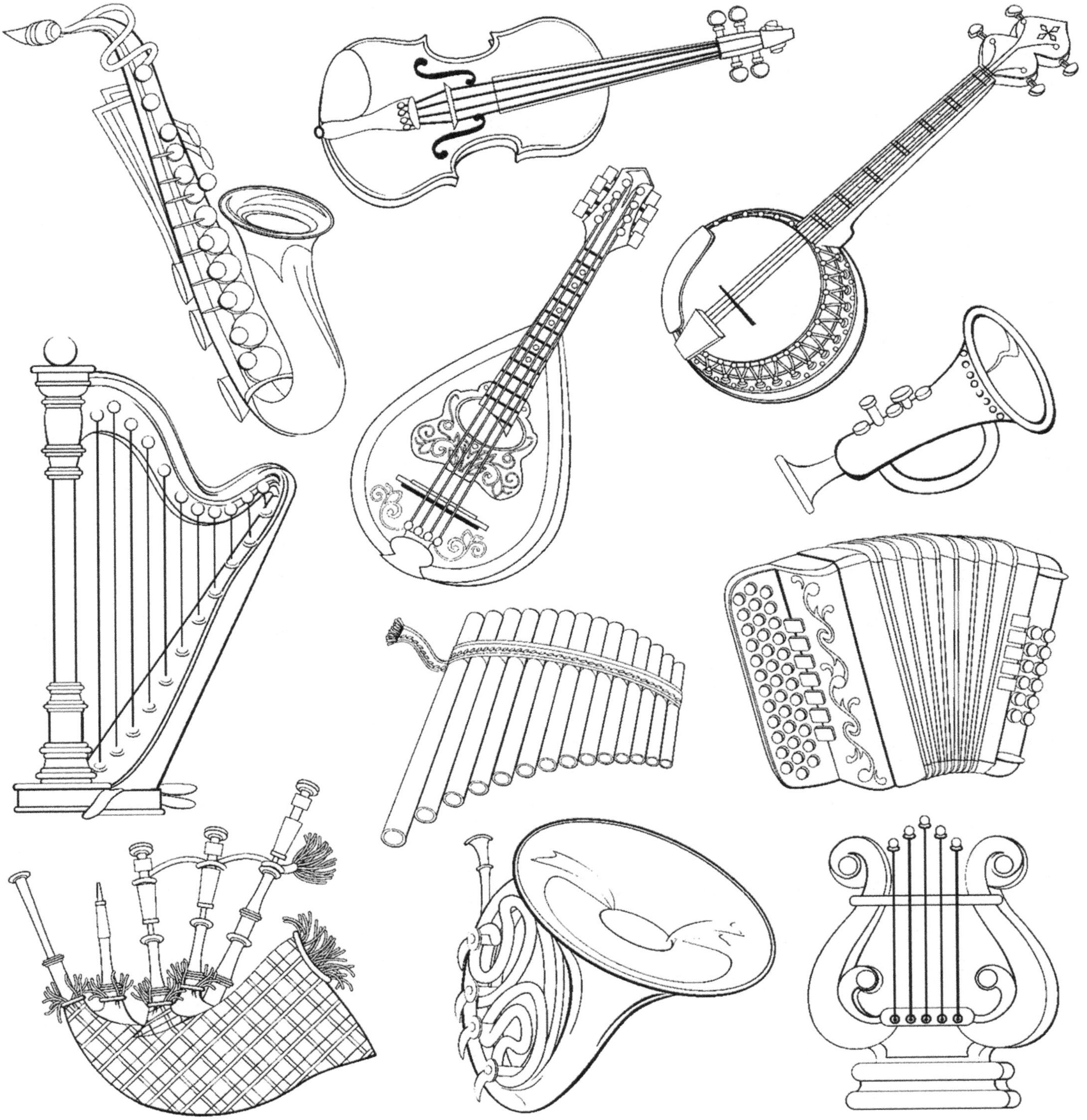

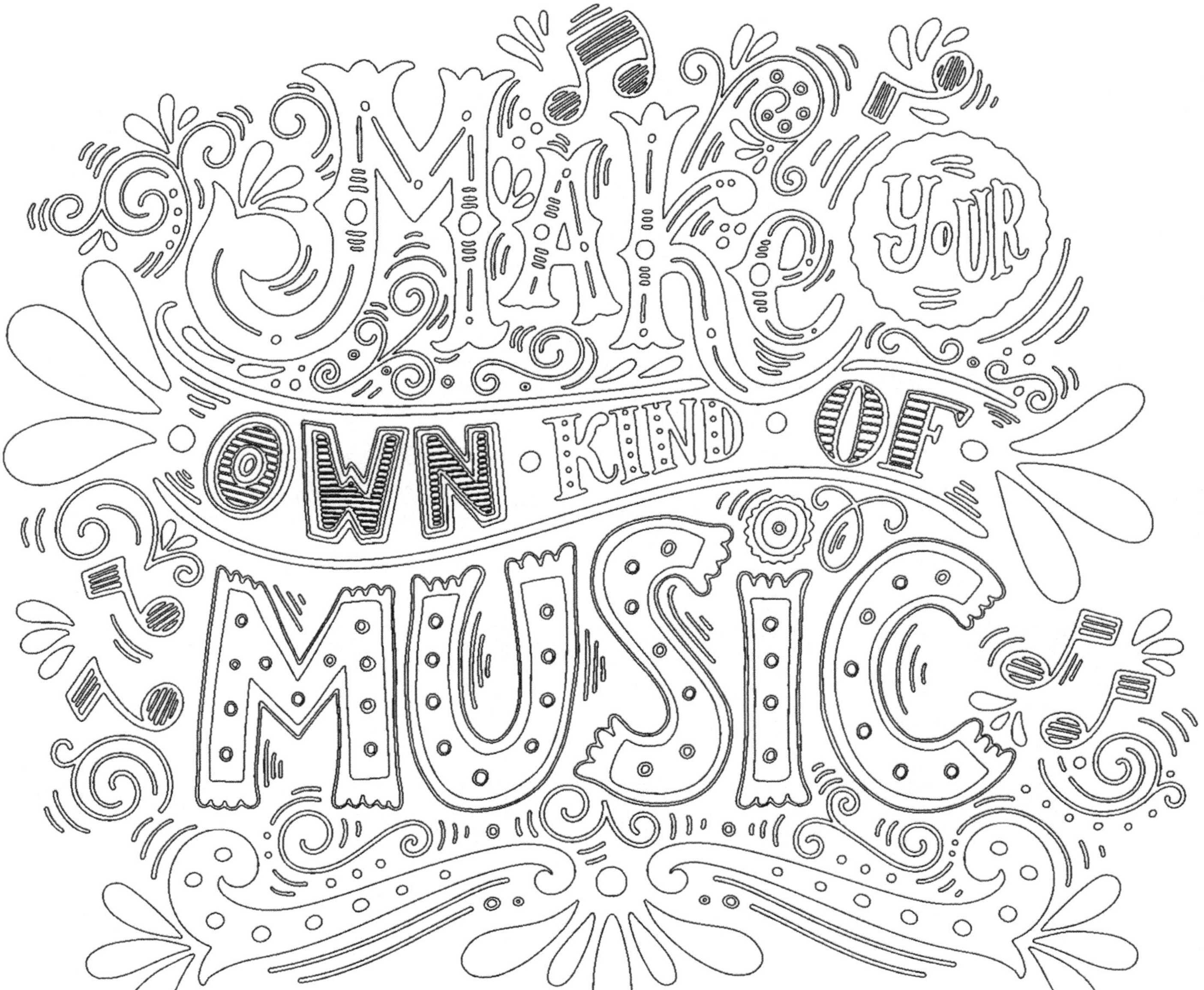
MAKE YOUR
OWN KIND OF
MUSIC

Made in the USA
Monee, IL
11 December 2020

52394239R00063